"Karpan comprehensively deals with education: preparing our students to courses cannot replicate future, real-li~~~ ~~~~~~~~~. Chapter by chapter, she systematically unpicks the complexities of programming and, in doing so, provides a framework for students that it is valuable, necessary and manageable."

Russell Gagg, *Principal Lecturer Interior Architecture and Design, Arts University Bournemouth*

"This textbook describes the background of programming that supports its use and, then, introduces students to a method especially suitable for lower division students. It provides an excellent companion to other programming related textbooks that allows upper division students to learn a wide-range of programming views before entering the workforce."

Linda L. Nussbaumer, *PhD, IDEC, NCIDQ*

"Strong, thoughtful programming is the foundation of effective design solutions. In this book, Cynthia has covered all the bases – both the theoretical and the practical in a narrative style that is informal and engaging. This will be an asset to students and teachers in developing designers with strong programming skills."

Carol Jones, *BID, RID, FIDC, FIIDA, ASID, LEED AP, DLitt*

PROGRAMMING INTERIOR ENVIRONMENTS

Programming Interior Environments introduces a four-component framework you can use to program interiors, and twelve methods for you to gather, analyze and synthesize programmatic information to take the guesswork out of your studio projects.

This book studies the Student Programming Model, a realistic programming process for college and university interior design students that allows students to create accurate and in-depth programming documents essential for informing the design process. This is done while keeping in mind that students are often working solo, with imaginary clients and end users in mind, and collecting program information within strict time constraints.

Including three appendices of student programs created following these guidelines, to help you understand how to apply the framework components and inquiry methods in your own work, this book is ideal for students and professionals in interior design and interior architecture.

Cynthia M. Karpan is an Associate Professor of Interior Design at the University of Manitoba in Winnipeg, Manitoba, Canada.

PROGRAMMING
INTERIOR
ENVIRONMENTS

A Practical Guide for Students

Cynthia M. Karpan

Routledge
Taylor & Francis Group

NEW YORK AND LONDON

First published 2020
by Routledge
52 Vanderbilt Avenue, New York, NY 10017

and by Routledge
2 Park Square, Milton Park, Abingdon, Oxon, OX14 4RN

Routledge is an imprint of the Taylor & Francis Group, an informa business

Library of Congress Cataloging-in-Publication Data
Names: Karpan, Cynthia, 1964– author.
Title: Programming interior environments : a practical guide for students / Cynthia Karpan.
Description: New York : Routledge, 2020. | Includes bibliographical references and index.
Identifiers: LCCN 2019031406 (print) | LCCN 2019031407 (ebook) |
ISBN 9781138889675 (hardback) | ISBN 9781138889682 (paperback) |
ISBN 9781315712734 (ebook)
Subjects: LCSH: Interior decoration–Computer-aided design–Textbooks.
Classification: LCC NK2114 .K37 2020 (print) | LCC NK2114 (ebook) | DDC 747.0285–dc23
LC record available at https://lccn.loc.gov/2019031406
LC ebook record available at https://lccn.loc.gov/2019031407

ISBN: 9781138889675 (hbk)
ISBN: 9781138889682 (pbk)
ISBN: 9781315712734 (ebk)

Typeset in Fairfield
by Newgen Publishing UK

CONTENTS

FIGURES

TABLES

ACKNOWLEDGEMENTS

Writing this book took two years more than I thought it would. So, over the years, I've had many assistant editors. Two, however, deserve special thanks. First, Wendy Fuller, Assistant Editor, Architecture, Routledge. Without her efforts in "pitching" this book to the powers that be, I would not be writing these acknowledgements. I'm thankful that Wendy and the powers that be were willing to take a chance on an unpublished author like myself.

Second, and most recently, Julia Pollacco. Assistant Editor, Architecture, Routledge. Julia, I appreciated your prompt answers to my never-ending questions – especially the ones that I peppered you with almost daily during the week before my deadline!

Russell Gagg, Course Leader, Interior Architecture and Design, Arts University Bournesmouth; Carol Jones, Principal, Kasian Architecture Interior Design and Planning Ltd., Vancouver, BC; and Linda Nussbaumer, Professor Emeriti of Interior Design, South Dakota State University. Thank you for endorsing this book even though the draft you received was horrendous! I was elated when each of you so quickly and enthusiastically agreed to write in support of the book.

Peter Insole, Principal Historic Environment Officer, Bristol City Council deserves thanks and acknowledgement for kindly providing a map of the Stokes Croft conservation area in Bristol, UK, and for providing permission to use that map, and another, in the *Blackthorn Live/Create* program (Appendix A).

Paisley Chesters, Permissions Co-Ordinator, John Wiley & Sons Limited deserves acknowledgement and thanks for providing permission to use, and alter, content from: Kriebel, Teresa M., Craig Birdsong, and Donald J. Sherman. 1991. "Defining interior design programming." *Journal of Interior Design Education and Research* 17 (1): 29–36.

Marvid and vasabii warrant thanks for making their artwork available through iStock.com and Adobe Stock respectively.

June Derksen of June Bug Design. Thank you, June not just for your graphic design expertise but for your kindness and support in my moments of panic. I appreciate the sense of calm that you exuded, and I appreciate the fact that you were able to fit my timeline into yours.

Shane Cuenca, Josh Lingal, and Tiffany Maybituin. Wow! Such talented, enthusiastic, and remarkably respectful individuals. I appreciate all of the hard work you put into formatting the sample program documents for the Appendices. In only your third year of university, the three of you show maturity beyond your years. Thank you for helping out your "old" professor when you were so very busy yourselves.

And last but certainly not least, a huge thank goes out to my good friend, Claire "Juxtaposition" Gregoire. The support and sustenance you provided throughout this long process was appreciated especially in the last three weeks of writing. I could not have done this without you, pal. BTW, you're an excellent proofreader!

Gem Gem, Stinker, Scooter, Nibs, McDuff, Smudge, Lily, Audrey, Duffy, and Pixie.

Chapter 1

INTRODUCTION

If this is the first book you've ever looked at about programming, then you need a bit of context. That is, you need to understand how the subject of programming interior environments fits with what you already know about interior design. If you've already read a book or two on programming, or done programming yourself, then you can consider this chapter just a little refresher about how programming fits within interior design.

To begin with, you might be wondering, "What is programming anyway? Is it a part of the design process? Do I have to write a program for every single design project that I do?" This chapter answers those questions and a few more; beginning with an explanation about why I wrote this book for students.

Intended Audience

This book was written because there are only a few publications available on programming interior environments. While there are plenty of books about architectural programming, it is only recently that Botti-Salitsky (2009) and Dickinson and Marsden (2009) published programming books specifically for the interior design discipline. Botti-Salitsky's (2009) book is strictly about programming, and Dickinson and Marsden's (2009) is about the relationship between programming and research. Additionally, a book by Nussbaumer (2009) is about evidence-based design which, of course, includes programming. In 1998, Scott-Webber published a book about programming interiors but it is not readily available from the publisher.

Undoubtedly, these books have contributed much to the growing body of literature on interior design processes, programming, and research methods. What this book adds to the interior design body of knowledge is a realistic programming process; a process that is geared specifically toward you, the student.

You might be an undergraduate or graduate student in a college or university interior design program. I wrote this book with you in mind because I recognized the need for a practical programming process – one that would help you produce a high-quality program in a reasonable amount of time, and one that would assume that you'll be working alone on your project with either real or hypothetical clients.

Instructors may find the book helpful as well because, in addition to the student-oriented programming process, the book includes an explanation about modern-day programming, when it emerged, and key moments in its evolution. Also included is an overview of recent interior design programming models. Instructors will find that the history, existing model analysis, and the Student Programming Model (SPM) provide an easy-to-understand theoretical foundation for teaching programming. Both students and instructors will find the programs included in the appendix useful as well since they were created using the process and methods described in this book. This practical and theoretical book can be used in both studio and stand-alone courses.

Programming

In interior design, programming is a pre-design activity that takes place prior to design development. This is true in both professional practice and design education. Programming is something you do before you start imagining design concepts or drawing bubble diagrams. Programming is a decision-making and priority-setting exercise that helps you identify the issues, problems, and needs that must be addressed in the eventual design solution. The process is also used to translate human needs and activities into physical space requirements, and to establish project objectives and design guidelines. Once you (or another designer) begins to generate design solutions, the project objectives and design guidelines help you make decisions and assess the degree to which your design solutions are consistent with the original project objectives.

Programming is a systematic and objective process for gathering, analyzing, and synthesizing information about a particular project. The process results in a program document. Some of you might think of the process as being labor intensive and unimaginative while others might think of it as an exciting and surprisingly creative process. Whether you consider it to be a mundane or creative activity, programming is necessary if you wish to save time (during the design phase), make informed decisions, and end up with a design solution that meets your client's goals and objectives or the objectives set out by your instructor.

Most post-secondary interior design programs in North America and the UK provide students with some form of instruction about programming whether that instruction takes place in a stand-alone course or a design studio. Regardless of where, when, or how it's taught, programming is an important part of interior design education that begins with an understanding of the overall design process.

The Design Process

Interior design practitioners, educators, and students don't all follow the exact same design process. That's because design is a creative activity. But, as Sam Kubba (2003, 65–66) explained:

Despite variations in techniques and terminology … the design methodology process has remained intact, consisting of seven sequential steps. These are:

1. Programming.
2. Schematic design.
3. Design development.
4. Construction documents.
5. Bidding (tendering) of construction documents.
6. Execution/supervision of project.
7. Post-occupancy evaluation.

Among other authors, Clemons (2017), Kilmer and Kilmer (2014), Pile (2003), Slotkis (2006) describe interior design processes similar to Kubba's (2003). So, if

Linear Design Process

Figure 1.1 Linear design process (content by author, illustration by June Bug Design)

Non-linear Design Process

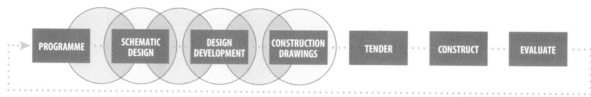

Figure 1.2 Non-linear design process (content by author, illustration by June Bug Design)

there is strength in numbers, then Kubba's (2003) model is an accurate reflection of the process used by most interior design practitioners and students.

As shown in Figure 1.1, the design process is often illustrated in a linear format. At the same time, most authors would agree that the actual design process doesn't always follow a strict linear format. Instead, designers sometimes go back-and-forth between various steps, or work on more than one step of the process at a time (Figure 1.2). It is notable, though, that the back-and-forth movement usually occurs in the early phases of the process rather than the latter. This is because once the design moves into construction documents and bidding, most of the decisions have already been made.

In real-life practice, interior designers complete all seven steps described by Kubba (2003). In university or college, however, you probably stop at step 3 or 4. Step 4, construction drawings, may or may not be required for your studio project. If construction drawings are not a part of your studio requirement, they may be required for your practicum or capstone project, or they may be done in a separate course. Steps 5–7 are not usually addressed in university or college because of the hypothetical nature of most studio projects, and because of time limitations with university or college semesters or trimester systems.

A noteworthy aspect of the design process is its inherent feed-forward characteristic. That is, the output or product of one step informs the next step. For instance, the product of step 3, design drawings, is used to begin step 4, construction drawings. Or, the outcome of a project (post-occupancy evaluation) leads to, or can inform, the beginning of a project (programming). These characteristics are evident in the SPM described in Chapter 3.

The Programming Process

Programming, the first step in Kubba's (2003) design process model, is more difficult to do in university or college than it is in real life. This is because, as a student, you are likely working alone, and you probably don't have real clients or end users to help you make decisions. Of course, you can always talk to your classmates but they are probably working on the same project as you. As such, your peers probably can't spare the time, or make the necessary mental shift between their project and yours, in order to provide you with the in-depth conversation or discussion necessary in order to achieve any kind of deep understanding.

Depending on your instructor, or on the nature of the project or assignment you are working on, you may need to generate imaginary clients and users along with imaginary project objectives; not easy tasks for seasoned interior designers to do let alone students. Sometimes, your instructor will provide you with client and end user profiles, or partial profiles but, in the end, it is still up to you to decide what the project objectives should be. In other words, you still have to pretend.

Some interior design and architectural books describe programming processes and methods that replicate those used in real-life practice. And, if the goal of education is to prepare students for real-life practice, then books about real-life programming methods make sense. Unfortunately, it is almost impossible for you to use real-life programming methods because such methods require access to real clients, or require group work that involves clients, programmers, designers, and maybe even others. In short, student programmers don't have available to them the resources available to practitioners.

Other interior design and architectural programming books describe research methods that can be used in programming. If you had plenty of time to complete your programming assignment, conducting research would be the ideal way to obtain original data to support your programming decisions. Again, most of you probably don't have time to conduct research that requires approval from your college or university human ethics board, and you most likely don't have time to conduct the type of data analysis that is expected when collecting original data.

This book responds to the student programming dilemma by offering the SPM. The SPM consists of a process and methods that will help you, the student programmer, complete your programming assignment with confidence and ease. The student model can be used with real or imaginary clients, end users, or buildings. The five-step process will guide you through information collection, analysis, synthesis, evaluation and revision, and communication that, in the end, will result in a program document for any type of interior project. Chapters 4–8, along with Appendices A- C, provide clear explanations, methods, and examples of how to use the SPM, and what your program document might look like.

The Program Document

A program document is the product that results from programming. Whether hard copy or digital, the document contains critical information about a project that has not yet been designed. It isn't a large binder stuffed with photocopied articles and endless notes, and it isn't an essay or novel. Instead, it is a concise document with short paragraphs, lists, charts, tables, diagrams, design drawings, images, and other project-related information.

The program's audience is the designer – one who will use the document as a guide to help him through conceptual and schematic design as well as design development. As a design student, you know that once you have your "design hat" on, the last thing you want to do is to have to stop and read a long document in order to find out what it is that you need to know. Instead, you want a quick reference – a chart or an image – that instantaneously provides you with the information you need. This is the program document.

The contents of a program document include background information on the client, factual information about the intended end users and their needs, project objectives and assumptions, informed estimates about spatial requirements and sizes, and design guidelines. In real-life practice, programs can also include information related to the budget and the timeline to project completion. In this book, and in most college and university interior design programs, neither budget nor timeline to occupancy issues are addressed because of the hypothetical nature of educational design projects.

In real-life practice, programs are fairly straightforward in that they are organized and professional looking documents. In university, students that I've taught seem to like unleashing their creativity with program documents using special layout or formatting software programs, and fonts and color that reflect the nature of their projects. How much time you spend on formatting the document is usually a personal choice, but your instructor may have certain requirements that need to be met as well. Regardless of the format, the document must be communicated well. Paying attention to things like spelling and grammar are important because they reflect your level of attention to detail and accuracy; attributes that good interior designers should have, and good programmers must have.

Programming Advantages

When faced with the challenge of your very first studio project, you probably generated countless design concepts, long lists of meaningful words, endless bubble diagrams, and several schematic sketches. You probably thought to yourself, "If I just keep drawing and writing, the solution will come to me." While this exhausting and stressful approach can be successful, it often results in a large pile of design options that are probably all interesting, appropriate, and creative enough, but are difficult to evaluate. Which concept, which schematic, which bubble diagram would best meet your client and end users' needs? What is it that you are really trying to achieve in your project? Programming can spare you such agony. Peña & Focke (1969, 6) explained that producing "sketch after sketch and plan after plan trying to satisfy undefined requirements ... [can lead to] a 'solution' to the wrong problem." A program can help you avoid solving the wrong problem by providing a well-investigated basis for design.

Botti-Salitsky (2009, 143) identified a second benefit of programming:

Students who have completed a comprehensive programmatic document enter the schematic design phase with less anxiety and more confidence. Typically the schematic design phase starts with lucid ideas that begin to take form from knowledge gleaned during the programming experience.

A third benefit of programming is that it can lead to innovative design solutions because programming provides you with an opportunity to re-think or challenge your own assumptions about end users' needs. Not all people live, work, and play the way you do. By investigating other peoples' characteristics, needs, and behavior patterns, you acquire the knowledge and evidence you need in order to challenge your own biases and justify your programming decisions. Marti (1981, 38) wrote that programming provides backup references and "sound reasoning that support design decisions thereby increasing the validity of the design solution."

Programming will help you save time, make design decisions with confidence, produce designs that meet specified objectives, reduce your stress level and anxiety during the design phase, and potentially lead you to an innovative design solution.

Programming Disadvantages

A great design program does not ensure a successful, innovative, or fantastic design solution. That's because the designer must interpret the program. If the program doesn't contain enough specific information and guidance, when it comes to the design phase, you, as the designer, may be forced to backtrack in order to collect and interpret more specific information. Having to backtrack is frustrating and time consuming. If you decide not to collect more specific information, then you risk producing a generic design solution that may not meet your own, your instructor's, or your hypothetical client and end users' needs.

Another programming weakness can be program documents that are too specific. In these situations, the designer, may feel "pigeon-holed" or "boxed in" in terms of creativity because the program is too specific. An example of this is one that I often share with students. It goes like this: If you know that your client needs storage for hanging garments, then in the programming phase, you should state how many linear feet of storage are required along with the minimum depth and height required. By stating the requirements this way (linear feet/meters and minimum depth and height), the designer has the opportunity to create an innovative solution for hanging garments. If the program states that the client requires a closet of a certain size, then the designer has little choice but to design a closet. In this example, the programmatic requirement of a "closet" limits the designer's ability to think creatively about how hanging garments could be stored.

Summary

Aimed at interior design students, this chapter provided context for interior design programming. The context was intended to help students understand how programming fits within the design process, what programming entails, and what some of programming's strengths and weaknesses are.

Besides context, the other important message in this chapter was that interior design students need a practical programming process. Students need a process that will help them create succinct, accurate, and useful programming documents in a reasonable amount of time.

Students need this practical process because, unlike professional practice where there are clients, end users, and colleagues to help with the programming process, in college and university, students must do all of the work by themselves and, they must play multiple roles while doing so. With hypothetical or imaginary clients and end users, students have to pretend that they are the client and make client decisions; they have to pretend that they are the end users and identify unbiased end user needs; they have to make decisions as a programmer; and they have to think about how the program is going to help them, or another designer, complete a successful design project. This is a heck of a lot of work for one student, and this is exactly why I created the SPM; a succinct practical programming process designed exclusively for you.

Chapter Overviews

Chapter 2 tells an interesting story of how modern-day programming came to be. The story begins in the late 1950s, and uses milestones to explain how and why programming became such an important part of the design process. Granted, in the first paragraph of the story, a drastic – but necessary – leap is made from the industrial revolution to the late 1950s, because it is the late 1950s that marks what many consider to be the modern era of programming.

Chapter 3 focuses on interior design programming and the SPM. The first part of the chapter describes seven interior design programming models that were selected from published literature, and that represent a variety of approaches to programming. After brief explanations about each model, the findings of an "informal and basic" analysis are explained. The major finding was that there is a remarkable similarity among the seven programming models; in fact, the similarities resulted in, ironically, a seven-phase generic programming model for interior design. This generic, amalgamated model is then compared to the five-phase SPM illustrating similarities and differences between the two. The remainder of the chapter explains what makes the SPM unique, and what the model consists of in terms of methods, topics, and products.

Chapter 4 gets into the core of the SPM. In this chapter, you'll discover the purpose and methods for information collection – the first phase in the SPM. You'll read about four simple methods for collecting information (read, interview, observe, record) on just two topics – your client's existing and desired conditions. Deceptively simple by name, these two conditions represent the entire essence of programming. The nice part about this phase is that you don't have to think too much – at least not in comparison to the next phase, analysis. Collecting all the information that'll you need to carry you through to the end of the program may sound like a daunting task and that's because it is. But, having all of the information on hand when you need it will save you a great deal of time and frustration down the road.

Chapter 5 addresses the second programming phase, analysis. In this chapter, you'll discover how to make sense out of all of the information you collected in phase 1. You might be surprised (and perhaps delighted) to know that the chapter describes just five simple methods for analyzing programmatic information: (a) dissecting text, (b) crunching numbers, (c) assessing, (d) annotating, and (e) drawing. You might be alarmed to know that these five methods have the potential to result in a lot of programmatic options. These options, however, are exactly what you'll want, and need, when you get to the third SPM phase, synthesis. Spoiler alert – synthesis results in your draft program document.

Chapter 6 is about synthesis, the third phase of the SPM. The chapter is an important one because it results in the draft program document. Here, the lone method for synthesis is constant comparison – a method used in qualitative data analysis. The chapter explains how constant comparison can be used to identify priorities which are needed to determine the content, and content order that will constitute your draft program document.

Chapter 7 addresses two topics – evaluation and revision, and communication. Often a dreaded part of most processes, the evaluate and revise phase of the SPM describes a short and simple process for ensuring accuracy in your final document. The second focus of the chapter, communication, addresses options for program content, organization, and formatting. The product resulting from evaluation, revision, and communication is the final program document.

The final chapter, Chapter 8, summarizes the SPM and reiterates my reasons for writing the book. As well, the summary identifies a few of the features that make the SPM unique. The chapter concludes with a few words about the future of programming, and about my steadfast belief that good programmers need empathy; something that technology, to date, has been unable to provide.

The three example programs included in Appendices A–C were created using the process and methods described in this book. The examples were designed to provide a range of programming contexts, project typologies, and geographic locations. The first program, *Blackthorn Live/Create*, is a renovation project in the UK for a hypothetical client, Kate Blackthorn. The second sample, *The HUB*, is a renovation and new construction project in Canada. *The HUB* is multi-purpose social and event space with a small bar and concession. The third program, *Extreme Toy Hauler Mobile Showroom*, is a new construction project located in the US.

References

Botti-Salitsky, Rose Mary. 2009. *Programming and Research: Skills and Techniques for Interior Designers*. New York: Fairchild.

Clemons, Stephanie A. 2017. *Interior Design*. Tinley Park, IL: Goodheart-Willcox.

Dickinson, Joan, and John P. Marsden, eds. 2009. *Informing Design*. New York: Fairchild.

Kilmer, Rosemary and W. Otie Kilmer. 2014. *Designing Interiors*. 2nd ed. https://bookshelf.vitalsource.com/#/books/9781118415801/cfi/6/2!/4/2/2/6@0:41.9

Kubba, Sam. 2003. *Space Planning for Commercial and Residential Interiors*. New York: McGraw-Hill.

Marti, Manuel Jr. 1981. *Space Operational Analysis: A Systematic Approach to Spatial Analysis and Programming*. West Lafayette, IN: PDA Publishers Corp.

Nussbaumer, Linda L. 2009. *Evidence-based Design for Interior Designers*. New York: Fairchild.

Peña, William, M. and John W. Focke. 1969. *Problem Seeking: New Directions in Architectural Programming*. Houston: Caudill Rowlett Scott.

Pile, John F. 2003. *Interior Design*. 3rd ed. Upper Saddle River, NJ: Prentice-Hall.

Scott-Webber, Lennie. 1998. *Programming: A Problem Solving Approach for Users of Interior Spaces*. Houston, TX: Dame Publications.

Slotkis, Susan J. 2006. *Foundations of Interior Design*. New York: Fairchild.

Chapter 2

MODERN-DAY PROGRAMMING

This chapter is about the evolution of modern-day programming since the late 1950s (Figure 2.1). While architectural literature provides most of the evidence for this chapter, there is a good reason why there is little published or available literature documenting the role of interior designers in the early years when programming was just emerging. Nonetheless, architectural literature provides valuable insight about why programming came to hold an important place in both architecture and interior design processes.

Changes to the architectural design process began, most noticeably, in response to the industrial revolution (circa 1760–1830). With the Industrial Revolution came advancements in technology, science, and ultimately, society. Throughout the decades and centuries since, revolutionary advancements resulted in people having more freedom and choice, and higher expectations than did their ancestors. This increasingly complex society desired increasingly complex buildings, and architects needed to figure out a way to respond to these new challenges. An article from a 1957 architecture journal provides an early indication of just how "modern day" architects planned to respond to the challenge.

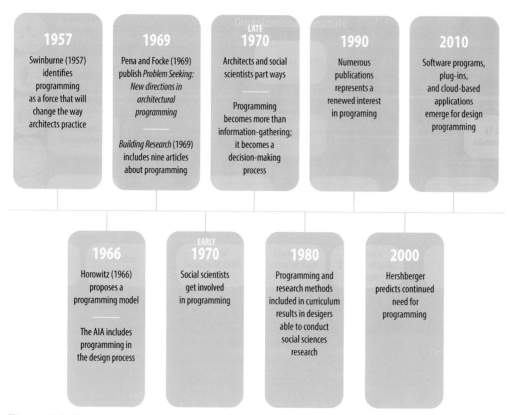

Figure 2.1 Key moments in the evolution of modern-day programming (content by author, illustration by June Bug Design)

1957

In 1957, Herbert Swinburne wrote an article for the *American Institute of Architects (AIA) Journal* called, "Change is the Challenge." Among other things, Swinburne identified programming as one of the "forces" that would change the way architects practiced. He wrote: "The impatient tendency to leap intuitively to a basic solution before a problem has been defined and all relevant facts researched and absorbed is now suspect" (Swinburne, 1957, 85). Swinburne's (1957) strong words captured what many architects already knew; in order to solve increasingly challenging commissions, they needed more than a "few notes on the back of an envelope" (Evans, 1969, 7), past experience, or intuition that many had relied on to date. Architects needed a more rigorous, systematic way of providing clients with "pre-design information" and obtaining "relevant, reliable, and comprehensible program data" (Palmer 1981, 276). Such a process would help architects create better solutions for complex projects and clients. Programming was to be that process.

Throughout the late 1950s and early '60s, numerous architects wrote articles about programming. They speculated about programming content, the process of programming, and who should program. Despite the many opinions expressed, there was little agreement about any of the issues. And, despite the growing urgency to use programming as a tool to solve complex projects, in the early 1960s, programming was still not included in the AIA design process; a process followed by many, if not most, architects at that time.

Mid 1960s

In 1967, Horowitz published an article called, "The Program's the Thing." He wrote that there remained three areas of confusion and disagreement with regard to programming: "1) responsibility for the program, 2) degree of program detail, and 3) program format" (Horowitz, 1967, 94). To address these issues, Horowitz proposed a programming model that he had actually published a year earlier (Horowitz, 1966). His model was not about how to program, but was, instead, a list of content that should be included in the program along with a format for programming. Horowitz's (1966, 72–73) content-oriented programming model is as follows:

1. Objectives of the master plan.
2. Special restriction and limitations on design.
3. Characteristics of the site.
4. Site development requirements.
5. Functional requirements for the facility.
6. Characteristics of the occupants.
7. Specific facility requirements.
8. Relative location and inter-relationship of spaces.
9. Budget.
10. Flexibility for future growth and changes in function.
11. Priority of need among the various requirements.

Although Horowitz's model is an important one, the more important consequence of his article was what the AIA did with it.

In 1966, the AIA revised their design process to include programming. The programming format and content that the AIA described was based on Horowitz's (1966) model, and was published in *Emerging Techniques in Architectural Practice* (American Institute of Architects, 1966). With the AIA's endorsement, programming had forever secured a place within the architectural design process.

In 1969, half of an entire issue of the *Building Research* journal was dedicated to the topic of programming. Edward Agostini (1969), Arthur Cogswell (1969), Gerald Davis (1969), Benjamin Evans (1969), Robert Gutman (1969), William Peña (1969), Stephen Richardson (1969), Richard Seaton (1969), and Douglas Sherman (1969) wrote articles about the value of programming and other related topics. It was clear that the architecture discipline had embraced the concept of programming. But, as with most things, the evolution or programming did not stop there. Some architects modified and improved the basic programming format endorsed by the AIA while others forged ahead developing their own programming processes. One of the most frequently referenced architects to develop a unique programming model (different from the AIA's) was William Peña.

1969

In 1969 William Peña and John Focke wrote an important book that described their unique approach to programming. The book was called, *Problem Seeking: New Directions in Architectural Programming*. Still in circulation today, the fifth edition of this book was published by Peña and Parshall in 2012.

Over the years, Peña and Focke's (1969) programming process has been modified, but the core process and content remain true to the original model. Noteworthy, from an interior design perspective, is the fact that the Council for Interior Design Qualification (CIDQ) (2019) includes Peña and Parshall's (2012) book on its list of recommended readings in preparation for taking the qualification exam. Peña and Focke's (1969, 14) process includes:

1 *Establish Goals*
2 *Collect, Organize and Analyze Facts*

3 *Uncover and Test Programmatic Concepts*
4 *Determine the Real Needs*
5 *State the Problem*

Up until the latter part of the 1960s, the evolution of programming was primarily due to internal efforts; that is, architects decided what programming should be, how it should be done, and who should do it. During the late 1960s, however, a group of individuals, external to architecture, came to play an important role in the direction programming would take for the next decade.

Late 1960s and Early 1970s

The late 1960s and early '70s marks a time when architects and social scientists first started collaborating on architectural programs. With the assistance of social scientists, architects could now design solutions that responded not only to the needs of clients who commissioned the projects, but also to the needs of the people who would inhabit the structures (end users) (Moleski, 1978). Architects were enthused about the potential ability to use the reliable and valid information generated by social scientists to help them (architects) justify their programming and design decisions.

Robert Hershberger (1999) explained how social scientists and architects came together. He wrote that, in the late 1960s, social and behavioral scientists from new disciplines called "environmental psychology, environmental sociology or human ecology" began to take an interest in architectural programming (Hershberger, 1999, 14). Individuals like Altman, Hall, Lawton, and Cooper Marcus came together with architects at the Environmental Design Research Association (EDRA) conferences. These social scientists, with their various methods such as "systematic observation, controlled interviewing, questionnaires and surveys, sampling, and statistical analysis … ushered in a time of extensive research oriented to developing knowledge about the environmental needs of various user groups" (Hershberger, 1999, 15).

Programming continued to flourish in the 1960s and '70s with numerous architectural firms specializing in programming services (White, 1972). Often, these firms had social scientists on staff. Other businesses opened up that offered programming services exclusively (no design services). Despite Palmer's (1981, 277) prediction that clients would demand "more sophisticated data analysis, and Farbstein's (1976, 24) suggestion that more stringent methods (i.e., empirical research), theoretical frameworks, and research were needed in order to make programming better, by the end of the 1970s, there were signs that architects had, perhaps, had their fill of social sciences researchers and scientific research methods.

Herring, Szigeti, and Vischer (1977) claimed that programming had become a process that required trained experts (social scientists or other researchers) to distill research data into criteria that a designer could understand and use. Other architects felt the same, and so it was not long before the architect/social scientist relationship fizzled out.

Late 1970s

One of the reasons that architects and scientists parted ways was that programming had become an information gathering process that resulted in huge amounts of data. McLaughlin (1978, 180) claimed that programming documents had become "too long, too complete, and too complex," and that such documents stifled "the creative synthesis of data that can result in the unusual design." Silverstein and Jacobson (1978) echoed McLaughlin's (1978) concern claiming that programming often resulted in functional, but sterile, buildings and interior environments.

A second reason for the failed relationship between architects and social scientists was that many architects were frustrated by their own inability to understand the methods, language, and results of social scientists. McLaughlin (1978, 187) said, "Architects are not very good at reading tables and deciphering social scientists' elaborations. We need translations …."

The third reason for the defunct relationship was the fact that, by now, architects realized that programming had lost its original intent, which was to challenge assumptions and stereotypes about end users and their needs (Silverstein and Jacobson, 1978). Instead, programming had become an information and data processing exercise.

On a positive note, during the 1970s, there was a small surge of programming publications. Books by White (1972) and Sanoff (1977), an edited book by

Preiser (1978), and an important book by Palmer (1981) contributed to the growing body of architectural programming knowledge.

Published in 1981, but likely written in the late 1970s, Palmer's book represents an important milestone in the evolution of programming because it marks the end of the early era of modern-day programming. Although probably not intended to mark the end of an era, Palmer's programming model does just that because it summarizes models by six early era authors including: Gerald Davis, Jay Farbstein, John Kurtz, Walter Moleski, William Peña, and Edward White. Palmer's (1981, 31) summary is as follows:

- Establish project goals
- Organize programming effort
- Investigate issues
- Integrate data
- Interpret information
- Instruct designer and client
- Evaluate results
- Recycle information

1980s

In the 1980s, architects and designers, along with design educators, showed increased levels of interest in programming. Consequently, during this decade, programming was integrated into an increasing number of design firms and educational programs. White (1991) provided ten reasons for the growing popularity of programming during this timeframe. Some of the reasons were: (a) clients expect programming services from architects; (b) architecture firms that provide programming have a competitive advantage over other firms; (c) programming enables projects to proceed smoothly and efficiently resulting in saved time and money for both the client and the firm; and (d) design outcomes are better with programming than without.

Palmer (1981) reported that, in the early 1980s, at least twenty-four architecture schools in the US offered programming courses as part of the curriculum. White (1991, 1) wrote: "The strong trend toward more attention to architectural programming in the architecture curriculum reflects the growth of this professional service and the demand for these skills in professional practice."

Despite the fact that no significant developments or advancements to the programming process were made during the 1980s, through the decade, programming continued to gain importance in the architecture and interior design disciplines. Architecture and interior design students were now being trained in social sciences research methods, and were well aware of the importance of research in terms of practicing evidence-based design. With programming and research methods cemented into curricula, future generations of architects and interior designers would be able to translate and decipher social sciences data themselves – a need identified by McLaughlin (1978) in the late 1970s.

1990s

By the early 1990s, programming had evolved from an information-gathering and organizing exercise (Heimsath, 1977) to a more comprehensive process that involved investigating and developing information, analyzing client and end user needs, and evaluating projects after construction and occupancy (Freidman, Zimring, and Zube, 1978).

During the 1990s, there was a small but significant number of books published about architectural programming. Books by Edith Cherry (1999), Donna Duerk (1993), Robert Hershberger (1999), Robert Kumlin (1995), and Henry Sanoff (1992) added to the growing body of programming knowledge and represented a new era of programming authors. Each of these new-era authors contributed advanced methods for collecting and analyzing information, and each espoused a particular view about how programming should be done. For the most part, however, none of the authors suggested revolutionary changes to the purpose of, or process for, programming.

During this time period, Scott-Webber (1998) was the only interior designer to publish a book about programming interior environments. Other interior design authors (Kilmer and Kilmer, 1992; Pile, 1995) included programming as a topic or chapter in their comprehensive books about interior design. Come the turn of the century, however, the interior design discipline finally saw a spike in programming publications.

2000–2010

In the early part of the twenty-first century, authors such as Allen, Jones, and Stimpson (2004), and Neilson and Taylor (2002) continued to publish comprehensive books about interior design. In varying degrees, each of these authors – and authors of similar books – made references to programming. From a programming evolution viewpoint, however, two interior design authors stand out – Karlen (2004) and Kubba (2003). The books written by these authors focused almost exclusively on programming interior environments – the only interior design authors to do so since Scott-Webber's 1998 publication.

At the end of the decade, two more important books were published that focused exclusively on programming interior environments. Botti-Salitsky (2009) and Nussbaumer (2009) each wrote comprehensive textbooks on programming – books that were needed, and that contributed substantially to the interior design body of knowledge. The next chapter describes programming models put forth by some of the interior design authors from this decade.

2010–2020

The one notable development in modern-day programming emerged somewhere around 2010 but maybe even earlier than that. This development was, as you may have guessed, computer software programs that could assist with architectural and interior design programming.

While I am by no means even slightly familiar with any of these programs, it seems to me that these software programs have the potential to speed up the programming process, and to make programming more accurate and consistent. This is because most of the programs rely on all of the project data being entered into a central database where the software helps perform "checks and balances" throughout the programming process, and the entire design process thereafter.

Summary

This chapter explained how modern-day programming evolved into the process that it is today. The explanation started with the 1950s when programming was conceived of as a way to help architects respond to increasingly complex clients and projects. Throughout the 1960s, architects generated a variety of models and methods for programming, but there was a general feeling that programming could result in even more valuable information than current models allowed.

In the 1970s, behavioral scientists became involved in the architectural programming process. Architects welcomed their involvement because these scientists had the research methods and data analysis expertise necessary for extracting deep meaning about human behavior in built environments. As designers and behavioral scientists experimented with different ways of making programming better, the unfortunate outcome was that programming became too complex.

After the relationship between social scientists and architects fizzled out, and after design schools began to incorporate research methods into post-secondary programs, architects began to take back control of programming.

Since the late 1980s, programming has not evolved tremendously – at least in terms of its purpose and outcome. What has changed, however, is the way programmers conduct programming. Since the 1990s, computer technology has enabled programmers to collect, analyze, and synthesize greater amounts of information with more accuracy than before and, more recently software programs have been developed to assist in architectural programming.

References

Agostini, Edward J. 1969. The value of facilities programming to the client. *Building Research*, 6 (2):28–32.

Allen, Phyllis Sloan, Lynn M. Jones, and Miriam F. Stimpson. 2004. *Beginnings of Interior Environments*. 9th ed. Upper Saddle River, NJ: Pearson Prentice Hall.

American Institute of Architects. 1966. *Emerging Techniques of Architectural Practice*. New York: The American Institute of Architects.

Botti-Salitsky, Rose Mary. 2009. *Programming and Research: Skills and Techniques for Interior Designers*. New York: Fairchild.

Cherry, Edith. 1999. *Programming for Design: From Theory to Practice*. New York: Wiley.

Cogswell, Arthur R. 1969. Programming and a computer-based cost analysis system. *Building Research*, 6 (2):33–35.

Council for Interior Design Qualification. 2019. *NCIDQ Exam Reference Materials*. www.cidq.org/study

Davis, Gerald. 1969. The independent building program consultant. *Building Research*, 6 (2):16–21.

Duerk, Donna. P. 1993. *Architectural Programming: Information Management for Design*. New York: Van Nostrand Reinhold.

Evans, Benjamin H. 1969. Building design programming. *Building Research*, 6 (2):7.

Farbstein, Jay. 1976. Assumptions in environmental programming. Vol. 28 of *The Behavioral Basis of Design Book 1: Selected Papers*, ed. L. M. Ward, S. Coren, A. Gruft, and J. B. Collins, 21–26. Stroudsburg, PA: Dowden, Hutchinson & Ross.

Friedmann, Arnold, Craig Zimring, and Ervin Zube. 1978. *Environmental Design Evaluation*. New York: Plenum Press.

Gutman, Robert. 1969. The sociological implications of programming practices. *Building Research* 6 (2):26–27.

Heimsath, Clovis. 1977. *Behavioural Architecture: Toward an Accountable Design Process*. New York: McGraw-Hill.

Herring, Barry, Francoise Szigeti, and Jacqueline Visher. 1977. Programming and environmental analysis in practice. In *The Behavioral Basis of Design Book 2: Selected Summaries and Papers* (Proceedings of the Seventh International Conference of the Environmental Design Research Association). Vancouver, BC.

Hershberger, Robert G. 1999. *Architectural Programming and Predesign Manager*. New York: McGraw-Hill.

Horowitz, Harold. 1966. The architect's programme and the behavioural sciences. *Architectural Science Review* 9 (3):71–79.

Horowitz, Harold. 1967. The program's the thing. *AIA Journal*, 47 (5):93–100.

Karlen, Mark. 2004. *Space Planning Basics*. 2nd ed. Hoboken, NJ: Wiley.

Kilmer, Rosemary and W. Otie Kilmer. 1992. *Designing Interiors*. Toronto, ON: Harcourt Brace.

Kubba, Sam. 2003. *Space Planning for Commercial and Residential Interiors*. New York: McGraw-Hill.

Kumlin, Robert R. 1995. *Architectural Programming: Creative Techniques for Design Professionals*. New York: McGraw-Hill.

McLaughlin, Herbert. 1978. User needs in residential areas: Martin Luther King Square, San Francisco. In *Facility Programming: Methods and Applications*, ed. Wolfgang F. E. Preiser, 179–198. Stroudsburg, PA: Dowden, Hutchinson & Ross.

Moleski, Walter H. 1978. Environmental programming for human needs. In *Facility Programming: Methods and Applications*, ed. Wolfgang F. E. Preiser, 107–126. Stroudsburg, PA: Dowden, Hutchinson & Ross.

Nielson, Karla J. and David A. Taylor. 2002. *Interiors: An Introduction*. 3rd ed. Boston: McGraw-Hill.

Nussbaumer, Linda L. 2009. *Evidence-based Design for Interior Designers*. New York: Fairchild.

Palmer, Mickey A. 1981. *The Architect's Guide to Facility Programming*. New York: The American Institute of Architects / McGraw-Hill.

Peña, William, M. 1969. Organizing for programming. *Building Research* 6 (2):8–11.

Peña, William, M. and John W. Focke. 1969. *Problem Seeking: New Directions in Architectural Programming*. Houston: Caudill Rowlett Scott.

Peña, William M. and Steven A. Parshall. 2012. *Problem Seeking: An Architectural Programming Primer*. 5th ed. Hoboken, NJ: Wiley.

Pile, J. F. 1995. *Interior Design*. 2nd ed. Englewood Cliffs, NJ: Prentice Hall.

Preiser, Wolfgang F. E., ed. 1978. *Facility Programming: Methods and Applications*. Ed. Richard P. Dober. Vol. 39, Community Development Series. Stroudsburg, PA: Dowden, Hutchinson & Ross.

Richardson, Stephen. 1969. The value of a program to the architect. *Building Research* 6 (2): 40–42.

Sanoff, Henry. 1977. *Methods of architectural programming*. Ed Richard P. Dober. Vol. 29, *Community Development Series*. Stroudsburg, PA: Dowden, Hutchinson & Ross.

Sanoff, Henry. 1992. *Integrating programming, evaluation and participation in design: A theory Z approach*. Ed. D. Canter and D. Stea. Vol. 6, Ethnoscopes: Current Challenges in the Environmental Social Sciences. Aldershot, England: Avebury.

Scott-Webber, Lennie. 1998. *Programming: A Problem Solving Approach for Users of Interior Spaces*. Houston, TX: Dame Publications.

Seaton, Richard. 1969. Research for building programming. *Building Research* 6 (2):36–39.

Sherman, D. R. (1969). Building programming at Wayne State University. *Building Research*, 6 (2):2–25.

Silverstein, Murray and Max Jacobson. 1978. Restructuring the hidden program: Toward an architecture of social change. In *Facility Programming: Methods and Applications*, ed. Wolfgang F. E. Preiser, 7–26. Stroudsburg, PA: Dowden, Hutchinson & Ross.

Swinburne, Herbert H. 1957. Change is the challenge. *AIA Journal* 47 (5):83–90.

White, Edward T. 1972. *Introduction to Architectural Programming*. Tucson, AZ: University of Arizona.

White, Edward T. 1991. *Teaching Architectural Programming*. Tucson, AZ: Architectural Media.

Chapter 3

INTERIOR DESIGN PROGRAMMING MODELS

Most of the previous chapter refers to architects and the architecture discipline. This chapter focuses on interior designers and the interior design discipline. Provided here are two overviews; one of seven published interior design programming models, and another of the Student Programming Model (SPM) that is the focus of this book.

Seven Interior Design Programming Models

The seven models discussed below were not selected because they are representative of all interior design programming models, but because they were readily available in published literature, and they demonstrate a range of approaches for programming interior environments. A basic and informal analysis of the similarities and differences between the models resulted in a number of interesting observations, and in a generic, or representative, programming model that I call an amalgamated model. Both results provide context to help you understand how the SPM fits with existing programming models.

A few words about my "basic and informal analysis." I confess, unabashedly, that all I did was combine all of the "steps" from each author's model to create one big model. Then, I reduced the model to seven steps that seemed to capture the essence of the majority of authors' models. In doing this, it was clear that two steps by Karlen (2004), and one step by Botti-Salitsky (2009) were the only three steps that were unique; that is, no other author identified them in his or her model. Out of the more than forty steps combined, I didn't feel bad omitting the three "outliers" from my seven-step model. Later in the chapter, I demonstrate how the seven-step amalgamated model compares with the five-step SPM, and with Kriebel, Birdsong, and Sherman's (1991) three-step model.

The second basic analysis I performed was to simply identify each author's main audience. I wanted to see if the intended audience had any impact on the models in terms of how the models were structured, what each model contained, or how each model was described. I discovered that five of the seven authors identified students, one identified practitioners and educators, and one identified practitioners as their target audiences.

Despite the different target audiences, the programming models are surprisingly similar. This finding suggests that the structure, content, and descriptions of interior design programming models for students are similar to programming models for practitioners. I was rather disturbed by this finding since it seemed to undermine the entire rationale for this book. What I realized, though, is that even though student and real-life programming processes may be similar, it is actually the methods of programming, and the people involved in creating the programs, that are different for students and practitioners.

A third analysis result is that the seven programming models are all what I call "hybrid" or "comprehensive" models because they describe the process, content, and methods for programming. This is contrary to early architectural programming models that tend to be process-driven, content-driven, or both process- and content-driven. Obviously, process-driven models, like Peña and Focke's (1969), describe a programming process that should be followed in order of the steps identified in the model. Content-driven models, like Horowitz's (1966), describe the content that needs to be collected, analyzed, or at least considered throughout the programming process. Process- and content-driven models, like White's (1972) describe both a process for programming as well as content that needs to be collected or generated for each programming phase. The differences between early

An Amalgamated Interior Design Programming Model

Familiarize & organize

Compile data

Analyze data

Interpret data (specify needs)

Evaluate

Organize & decide

Produce program document

Figure 3.1 An amalgamated interior design programming model (content by author, illustration by June Bug Design)

architectural programming models and the modern interior design programming models suggest that programming models have evolved since the late 1950s, and/or that interior designers today think about programming differently than did their counterparts over fifty years ago.

Knowing whether a programming model is process-driven, content-driven, both process-and content-driven, or a hybrid is not all that important but it is something to be aware of if you're a student or young practitioner trying to decide which programming model to follow. Do you prefer a loose process framework to guide you through programming, or do you need something more detailed, like the combined process-and content-driven, or hybrid, models? Clearly, there are many models to choose from.

The fourth, and final, result of my analysis is this. Despite the fact that almost thirty years separate the first and last models, in my opinion, there are no remarkable differences between them. This finding suggests that the amalgamated interior design programming model (Figure 3.1) reflects a relatively stable programming process in the interior design discipline. Whether or not technological advancements will affect future programming models is unclear, but my guess is that the methods for collecting and analyzing information are more likely to change rather than the programming process itself.

With the analysis of existing interior design programming models complete, it's time to learn about the SPM. The next part of the chapter provides an overview of the model – including methods and products – but begins with a brief explanation of how the SPM fits with the amalgamated programming model (Figure 3.1) and with the extremely succinct model by Kriebel, Birdsong, and Sherman (1991).

Student Programming Model Overview

The SPM was designed to help you complete your own program. A hybrid model, the SPM consists of four components and five phases. Figure 3.2 shows the four components on the far left: process, topics, methods, and products. The second row shows the five phases: collect, analyze, synthesize, evaluate and revise, and

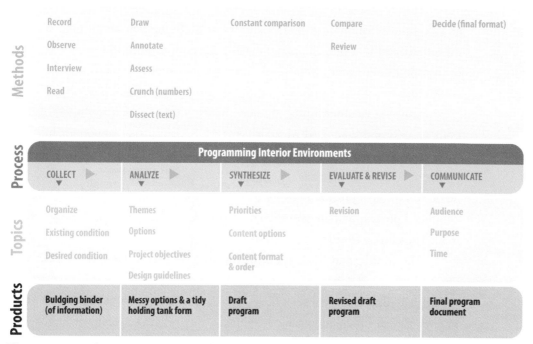

Figure 3.2 Student programming model (content by author, illustration by June Bug Design)

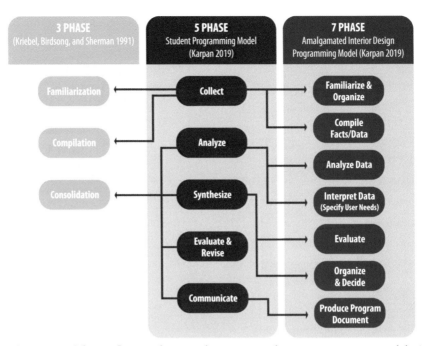

Figure 3.3 Three-, five-, and seven-phase interior design programming models (content by Kriebel, Birdsong, and Sherman, 1991; and author; illustration by June Bug Design; three-phase model adapted from Table 1, p. 35 in Teresa M. Kriebel, Craig Birdsong, and Donald J. Sherman, 1991. "Defining interior design programming." *Journal of Interior Design Education and Research* 17 (1): 29–36. Copyright, 1991. Interior Design Educators Council, *Journal of Interior Design Education and Research* 17 (1): 29–36).

communicate. Subsequent chapters provide detailed information about each component and phase of the model.

Before moving on to the SPM, a quick look at three programming models, side-by-side, is warranted. As shown in Figure 3.3, the five-phase SPM sits rather nicely between Kriebel, Birdsong, and Sherman's (1991) three-phase model and the seven-phase amalgamated model shown earlier (who knew that odd-number programming models were a thing?). Showing the three models, side-by-side, demonstrates how each model uses different language but essentially describes a similar process. Also noteworthy is the fact that Kriebel, Birdsong, and Sherman's model is intended for educators and practitioners, the SPM is for students, and the amalgamated model is for all three audiences. Again, despite the different audiences, no distinguishable difference exists between the models in terms of content, process, or vocabulary. And finally, I like seeing Kriebel, Birdsong, and Sherman's model in relation to the other two, because even without all of its detail, the abbreviated version of the authors' model succinctly captures the entire interior design programming process.

Student Programming Model

And now, on to the main purpose of this book – the SPM. The model was inspired by numerous programming authors, and over twenty years teaching interior design programming and studio courses. One author, in particular, influenced my approach to teaching programming. For me, Duerk (1993, 9) captured the essence of programming when she said that programming involves analyzing the "existing state" and "future state." In the SPM, you will see a clear distinction between existing and desired conditions, and I'm hopeful that you will come to appreciate Duerks' deceptively simple explanation about programming.

If you're using the SPM to create your very first program ever, you'll probably follow the model step-by-step, and address most, or all, of the topics associated with each phase. If you're a more experienced programmer, you may skip some of the suggested topics if you decide that they aren't relevant to your particular project. Which parts of the SPM you use, and which topics you address, depends on the nature of the project that you're programming, the amount of time you have, and your instructor's or client's expectations.

Features of the SPM include the following:

1. The model assumes that you are both the programmer and the designer. In real-life practice, the programmer and the designer may be different people or groups of people.
2. The model is designed to help you complete your program alone. This is because, in university and college, most of you work alone on your course or studio assignments. The process can be used for "group" or "team" programming as well though.
3. The process is designed for students who have little or no experience programming but contains information useful for those who have programming experience as well.

4. The SPM is based on assumptions that the environment you're programming will never be built, that you do not have a budget, and that you do not have real clients or end users with whom to discuss the program. The process, however, can be used even if you do have a real budget or client.
5. Just like the design process described in Chapter 1, the SPM is a feed forward model in that the outcome, or product, of one phase informs the next phase.
6. The SPM stresses people and activities as the basis for making programmatic decisions, and communicating programmatic information.

Over the years, the idea of activity-based programming seems to have been replaced with a "room data sheet" approach. While it's true that, in certain cases, room data sheets are appropriate, they tend to remove the "humanness" from programming. And yet, "humanness" is one of the principle foundations of modern-day programming. In the 1960s, Haviland (1967) and Moore (1969) promoted activity-by-activity programming rather than space-by-space programming. And, Moleski (1978) pointed out that preconceived building typologies, spaces, ideas, and intuition – no matter how well-informed – do not take into account individual needs and activities. Instead, pre-conceived building typologies and spaces emphasize national standards, pre-conceived forms, and generalizations about spatial purpose and human behaviour.

7. Closely related to the previous point, another feature of the SPM is one that I haven't seen discussed much in recent publications. Adopted from Silverstein and Jacobson (1978), this SPM feature promotes programming as a catalyst for change.

Lamenting about what they perceived as stereotypical buildings, Silverstein and Jacobson (1978) wrote that properly written programs can be catalysts for social change but, in order for change to occur, standards and existing knowledge must be challenged. Programmers who re-think context, purpose, and form can create truly innovative programs because they don't take anything for granted. These programmers take the time to collect and analyze a lot of information; put aside their own preferences, biases, and assumptions; and re-imagine how end users might function within a space. These are programmers who use programs to create change.

Programs based on generalizations can, and usually do, result in interior environments that meet the needs of clients and end users, but a program based on an in-depth understanding of client and end user needs and activities has greater potential to result in an innovative interior environment that surpasses client or end user expectations. For example, if you conduct a thorough investigation into the entire restaurant dining experience (entering, sitting, ordering food, paying the bill and exiting), and focus on how the experience could be improved, then it may be possible to envision a completely different and innovative dining experience. This new dining experience, conceived of and proposed in the program, would be the result of thinking, deeply, about human experiences and activities related to dining, rather than thinking about dining spaces as they exist currently.

8. The SPM includes both analysis and synthesis. Numerous interior design and architecture authors (Peña & Focke, 1969; Kilmer & Kilmer, 2014) state that programming is analysis while design is synthesis. Without synthesis, however, the program is simply a collection of information that is informative but does not provide the designer with any real direction in terms of design development. Synthesis is a form of decision-making and information reduction that is critical to successful programs because it reduces the number of decisions that need to be made later on in the design process. Synthesized statements and information such as project assumptions and objectives, and design guidelines can be used to test, compare, and evaluate potential design solutions (White, 1972, 16–17).

   The SPM can be used to program all sizes of projects from small to large. It can be used for projects that are abstract and conceptual in nature, as well as those that are concrete and pragmatic. It can be used for projects where you have real clients and buildings; projects where you do not have real clients or buildings; or projects where you have a combination of some real elements and others that are imaginary, hypothetical, or conceptual. The process can be used to program almost any scenario imaginable because it is a flexible process with topics and methods that can be adapted to suit your particular project. You decide which parts of the process, which content, and which methods to use depending on the nature of your project. The only real-life aspect that the SPM does not address is budget.

Summary

This chapter described seven interior design programming models and some of the similarities and differences between them. Even though differences exist in wording, intended audiences, and the number of steps in each model, among the seven models the basic programming process is similar. This conclusion mirrors the one that Palmer (1981) arrived at with early era architectural programming models described in Chapter 2; a conclusion which suggests that interior designers agree about at least two things – design and programming processes.

The second part of this chapter provided an overview of the SPM; a model that consists of four components (methods, process, topics, and products), and five phases (collect, analyze, synthesize, evaluate and revise, and communicate). Figure 3.2 showed the model in its entirety, and subsequent chapters describe each of the SPM components and phases.

References

Botti-Salitsky, Rose Mary. 2009. *Programming and Research: Skills and Techniques for Interior Designers*. New York: Fairchild.

Duerk, Donna. P. 1993. *Architectural Programming: Information Management for Design*. New York: Van Nostrand Reinhold.

Haviland, David S. 1967. The activity/space, a least common denominator for architectural programming. Paper presented at the AIA Architect-Researcher Conference, Gatlinburg, TN. https://eric.ed.gov/?id=ED018966

Horowitz, Harold. 1966. The architect's programme and the behavioural sciences. *Architectural Science Review* 9 (3):71–79.

Karlen, Mark. 2004. *Space Planning Basics*. 2nd ed. Hoboken, NJ: Wiley.

Kilmer, Rosemary and W. Otie Kilmer. 2014. *Designing Interiors*. 2nd ed. https://bookshelf. vitalsource.com/#/books/9781118415801/cfi/6/2!/4/2/2/6@0:41.9

Kriebel, Teresa M., Craig Birdsong, and Donald J. Sherman. 1991. Defining interior design programming. *Journal of Interior Design Education and Research* 17 (1):29–36.

Moleski, Walter H. 1978. Environmental programming for human needs. In *Facility Programming: Methods and Applications*, ed. Wolfgang F. E. Preiser, 107–126. Stroudsburg, PA: Dowden, Hutchinson & Ross.

Moore, Ian. 1969. Design methods and development programming. In *Design Methods in Architecture: Architectural Association Paper No. 4*, ed. G. Broadbent and A. Ward, 22–30. London, UK: Lund Humphries.

Palmer, Mickey A. 1981. *The Architect's Guide to Facility Programming*. New York: The American Institute of Architects / McGraw-Hill.

Peña, William, M. and John W. Focke. 1969. *Problem Seeking: New Directions in Architectural Programming*. Houston: Caudill Rowlett Scott.

Silverstein, Murray and Max Jacobson. 1978. Restructuring the hidden program: Toward an architecture of social change. In *Facility Programming: Methods and Applications*, ed. Wolfgang F. E. Preiser, 7–26. Stroudsburg, PA: Dowden, Hutchinson & Ross.

White, Edward T. 1972. *Introduction to Architectural Programming*. Tucson, AZ: University of Arizona.

Chapter 4

COLLECTION

The quantity and quality of information collected during phase 1 affects every subsequent programming phase and decision that you make. Given the importance of this phase, you're best to spend as much time as possible collecting the widest and deepest range of information possible. This advice applies to every programming project whether you have real or imaginary clients, spaces, or budgets.

Overview

You'll begin the programming process by collecting information on your client's existing and desired conditions. This chapter explains the purpose, rationale, methods, and sources for collecting information on these two topics, along with the products that result from this activity. At the end of the chapter, four lists summarize all of the information collection topics, methods, sources, and products described in the chapter.

Numerous examples are included throughout the chapter to help you understand some of the concepts and ideas explained. Some of the examples resulted from the **process** of creating the three program examples in Appendix A-C, while others are from the final program documents themselves. A quick explanation about the sample programs. They are all hypothetical, the content was created by me, and the creative formatting was done by three third-year interior design students. The

Blackthorn Live/Create residential program is in the UK (Appendix A). *The HUB* (Appendix B) is a multi-purpose event facility in central Canada. And, the *Extreme Toy Hauler Mobile Showroom* (Appendix C) project is located in the US.

Before running off to collect information, it's best to take a few minutes to get organized. Being organized is essential for ensuring that your information collection journey proceeds as smoothly as possible. Without having an organizational framework in place (and **following** the framework), as the information begins to pile up, you could very quickly become overwhelmed and frustrated.

Organize

In the three programming examples (Appendices A–C), I initially thought that I would collect all of the information and organize it in digital files on my laptop. However, some of the information I collected was not digital which meant that I would have to scan it in order to upload it onto the computer. I also thought that information analysis would be more difficult on the computer because, on my small laptop screen, proper analysis would require a lot of back-and-forth movement between documents and software programs. In the end, I found it easiest to print hard copies of everything and organize my information in good old-fashioned binders.

I had one binder for each program. Each binder had two main sections; one for the existing condition and one for the desired condition. Additional tabs were used to separate various sub-topics within the two main topics.

One situation that you might find yourself in while organizing information is when you've collected a document that could be placed into numerous categories or sub-categories. When this happens, you have two options. One, place the information into the category that you think best captures the main idea of the information. Two, make numerous copies of the information and place it in as many sections or sub-sections as is necessary. I prefer the latter option because it ensures that each section is self-contained which, in turn, reduces the need to flip back-and-forth during analysis.

For example, in the *Extreme Toy Hauler Mobile Showroom* program (Appendix C), I came across an article that could have been placed in either the "trends" or "people" category within the desired condition section of the binder. Instead of forcing myself to decide which category was the best fit, I simply made two copies of the article and placed one in each section. I should mention that, when I place the same article in more than one section, I jot down the location of the other copies on the top right corner of each copy. That way, I am aware of the fact that there is more than one copy in the binder.

The benefit of organizing your information into sections and sub-sections is that it's easy to identify gaps or missing information. This even more the case when using binders as opposed to digital files because, with binders, the empty sections are glaringly evident. While every single sub-section of your binder doesn't need to contain information, it is worth thinking about whether or not empty sections of the binder require further information gathering. Whatever gaps you find, and deem to be important, you should fill before moving onto phase 2, analysis.

Before jumping into analysis, however, let's collect some information. Again, the focus here is collecting information that will help you answer two questions. What is your client's **existing** condition, circumstance, or situation; and what is your client's **desired** condition, circumstance, or ideal situation?

Existing Condition

The point of documenting information about your client's existing design condition is to understand why your client asked you to design a new interior environment. What is your client hoping to achieve in the new environment? What problems exist with your client's current environment? What are the successful components or aspects of your client's existing space – things that your client would like to "carry over" into her new space? Answers to these questions, and many others, will help you either understand your real client's problems and expectations, or help you decide what your imaginary client's problems and expectations will be. Your instructor may have already made some of these decisions for you, but if you are a senior student fabricating your own scenario for a capstone, practicum, or thesis project, then you'll need to address these questions and make up some imaginary answers.

To understand your client's existing circumstances, you need to collect information on: (a) people, (b) workflow, (c) products, (d) the site, and (e) the building and space.

People

In the Student Programming Model (SPM), "people" includes owners, clients, and the end users who currently use your client's facility. Some owners may have little to do with the programming of a new facility. Instead, these owners might have an advisory board act as their representative which, for you, means that the advisory board is your client. Other owners may be very much involved in the programming of their new facility or environment. In these cases, owners – acting alone or with others – are your clients.

In any of these situations, owners, clients or owner/clients may not be end users. That is, owners, clients, or owner/clients will have a vested interest in the space that you're programming even though they, themselves, won't actually use the facility. Regardless of who constitutes your client, the client is the decision maker throughout the entire programming process.

End users, or occupants, are the individuals who will use the designed space when it's completed. End users often include employees; your client's customers or clients; the public; or other individuals.

Information that you collect on clients and end users will eventually be developed into descriptions and profiles. If you don't have real clients or end users, you can create client descriptions and end user profiles by inventing characters or job descriptions, or both. Using your imagination, you can create characters based on authors, poets, sports figures, celebrities, artists, individuals in the media, characters from books you've read, or any other source that inspires you or that seems appropriate for the project. When fabricating end users in particular, keep in mind that the more specific you can be about their personalities, preferences, or job descriptions, the easier it will be to make programming decisions later on.

In this early programming phase, you don't need to worry about how the client and end user information is formatted. Just make sure that you collect the information and keep it all together in your binder or digital file folder. You'll create the actual client descriptions and end user profiles in phase 3 when you create your draft program.

The type and amount of information that you need to collect about existing people depends on your project. You always want to collect information about your client, but collecting information about existing end users may or may not be necessary. You'll only collect end user information if the end users in the existing condition are going to be the end users in the desired condition. In most cases, they are one and the same.

Although your client's business, company, or organization is clearly not a person, a description of your client's business is normally included with the client description, or constitutes the client description in and of itself. You can fabricate a hypothetical business by creating one from imagination, or by amalgamating information from several real companies. Whether real or imaginary, the client description should include:

- Company, organization, or business name
- Address
- Client name
- Client contact information
- Company description
- Brief history of the company
- Company vision, mission statement, core values, and business objectives
- Organizational structure (Figures 4.1, 4.2)
- Future plans for growth
- Project goals

Beyond the company or business description, it may be worthwhile to collect (or fabricate) information about the actual client or clients themselves. What I mean in particular, is, "What are your client's values?" The reason values are important is because they can influence decisions. The more aware you are of your client's values, the more likely you will be able to predict how your client might respond to certain ideas or suggestions. If you don't have real clients, imagining values can be difficult so don't worry too much if you skip this exercise.

In single family residential projects, you'll likely have just one or two clients. In these situations, rather than collect information about your clients' business, you'll collect detailed end user information like that described shortly. This is because, in single family residential projects, your clients are most likely going to be end users as well as clients. If you're programming a multi-family dwelling,

Organizational Structure

President & CEO

VP Research & Development | VP Financial | VP Office Administration

VP Production ↔ VP Sales ↔ VP Marketing | Manager IT | Manager Human Resources

Director Parts Procurement | Director Assembly | Regional Director of Sales Asia | Regional Director of Sales North America | Regional Director of Sales Europe | Manager Facilities | Customer Service

Figure 4.1 Traditional hierarchical organizational structure for a motorcycle manufacturer (content by author, illustration by June Bug Design)

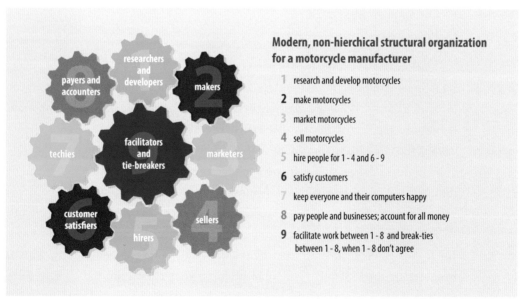

Modern, non-hierchical structural organization for a motorcycle manufacturer

1 research and develop motorcycles

2 make motorcycles

3 market motorcycles

4 sell motorcycles

5 hire people for 1 - 4 and 6 - 9

6 satisfy customers

7 keep everyone and their computers happy

8 pay people and businesses; account for all money

9 facilitate work between 1 - 8 and break-ties between 1 - 8, when 1 - 8 don't agree

Figure 4.2 Modern non-hierarchical organizational structure for a motorcycle manufacturer (content by author, illustration by June Bug Design)

however, you will want to treat your client in the same way as any other commercial or corporate client.

In interior design, end users (sometimes called occupants) are usually identified as being either primary, secondary, or tertiary. This designation relates to the frequency with which users occupy or use a space. So, primary users are those who use a space the most frequently while tertiary users are those who occupy the space least frequently. Within these three classifications, there can be numerous sub-groups. For example, primary users in a commercial project may consist of managers, assistants, and clerical workers. Tertiary users might include janitorial staff, couriers, and the public. Each of these sub-groups have different needs and engage in a variety of activities. Therefore, each end user, and sub-group, should have a distinct profile. Finally, profiles are more detailed for primary end users, less detailed for secondary end users, and even less for tertiary end users.

For primary end users, the more detailed the profiles, the more information both you and the eventual designer will have. More, rather than less, information is really helpful in terms of making programming decisions. That said, if you're programming a project in which there are more than 6–10 primary end users, you won't have time to document or invent detailed profiles for all of them. In this situation, you are better off to group end users into categories and then create a profile for each category. Grouping people into categories based on job description, activities, or even age and gender is sometimes necessary. For primary end users, real or imaginary, profile information that you should collect includes:

- Job or position title (or some other classification)
- Job status (full-time, part-time, contract)
- Number of end users who hold each job title
- Total number of primary end users
- End user activities or job responsibilities and tasks
- Frequency and duration of activities
- Degree of visual privacy required
- Degree of acoustic privacy required
- Special and/or future needs
- Gender, age, or other demographic information that could impact programmatic decisions

If you have less than 6–10 primary end users, or if you are designing for a special population, you may also need and want to collect information such as:

- Anthropometric data
- Physiological needs
- Psychological needs
- Traits/characteristics/personality
- Values
- Aesthetic preferences

Information needed for secondary or tertiary end user profiles is similar to that of primary end users but not nearly as detailed. You'll want to collect or document information on:

- The type of end user (secondary or tertiary)
- The number of secondary and tertiary end users in each sub-group and overall
- End user activities
- Frequency and duration of activities
- Special and/or future needs
- Gender, age, or other demographic information that could impact programmatic decisions

Workflow

Workflow refers to both individual and company processes that occur in your client's existing facility. The way a company operates is sometimes called "systems analysis" or "operational analysis." I prefer the word "workflow," and I like to leave out the word "analysis" since analysis occurs in the second phase of the SPM. I also include individual workflow which, refers to the way one person, or a group of people, work, engage, or communicate.

When collecting information about your client's operation, you can simply ask your client, or observe, how the company goes about doing its business; how daily operations or routines occur. What are typical company procedures? Does a workflow diagram (Figure 4.3) exist? Is there a certain order in which your client's product is made or services provided? To whom does your company sell its products or services?

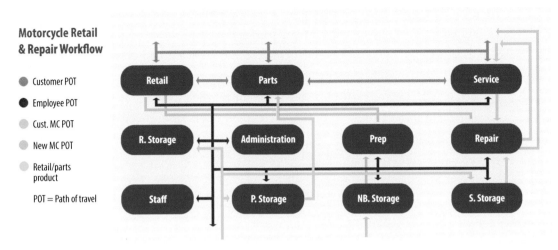

Figure 4.3 Motorcycle retail and repair business workflow diagram (content by author, illustration by June Bug Design)

Information on company processes is usually easy enough to collect and understand because companies often have descriptions of how the company is supposed to operate (i.e., the workflow diagram). Information on individual processes is not easy to collect, though, because doing so requires you to spend long hours observing end user interactions. Being that you're a student with limited time and, most likely, hypothetical clients, observation of end user activities and interactions is not realistic.

You do need, however, to understand how each end user group (and sub group) goes about its activities and work. Do end users have a daily routine? If so, what is it? Does the routine ever change? If so, when and why? You also need to collect information about how end users engage with one another. Do employees meet face-to-face, communicate via email or text, or talk to one another on the phone? How often, where, when, and with whom does this communication take place? This is where an organizational chart can be useful at least as a starting point.

Collecting all of this information may seem a bit overwhelming. The point of collecting it, though, is to gain a deep understanding of individual and procedural work flows, processes, or operations so that you can program a space that will satisfy your client's needs and expectations.

As a student, you won't have time to fabricate detailed information about the company or end user groups. If you can, at least fabricate your client's workflow, and make some generalizations about how employees communicate and engage with one another. It doesn't really matter what you decide in terms of company or individual processes; what matters most is that you document the processes. Later on, you and your client (or just you) can decide if company or end user processes should remain the same or change.

The more information you have about your client's workflow and processes (organizational and individual), the greater will be your understanding, and the more accurate will be your decision-making when programming your client's desired condition.

Products

Products are the things or services that your client produces, sells, or offers to their clients or customers. As a programmer, becoming familiar with your client's products is especially important if the products are ones that you're not familiar with. For example, if you were the programmer for the *Extreme Toy Hauler Mobile Showroom* (Appendix C), and if you didn't know what a toy hauler was, you would probably ask your client for sales brochures or pamphlets, review the company's website to see the company's products, and maybe even delve into products produced by companies other than your client's (i.e., the competition).

In some cases, your client's company or organization may sell a service rather than a product; however, the same questions apply. Find out, or fabricate, as much as you can about what those services are, how customers receive those services, and what services the competition offers. Knowing what the competition offers may be useful later on when you and your client are determining whether or not your client's workflow should change, or when you're trying to determine project objectives.

All of the information you collect about your client's products or services will provide you with a broad and unbiased understanding about your client's industry as a whole. This understanding is crucial if you are to program a space that will meet, and possibly exceed, your client's expectations.

Site

Not surprisingly, understanding your client's existing site contributes to your overall knowledge about your client's existing condition. If you have a real client, knowing whether she is staying at the existing site or moving to another is really helpful at this point because it affects the type and amount of information you'll collect. Regardless, it's good practice to document at least some information about the existing site.

Assuming that your client is remaining in her existing site, information that you should record includes:

- A site plan with scale and orientation (North, South, East, West) noted
- A building roof plan with main entrances identified
- Major streets, rivers, lakes, etc.
- Access to the site – vehicular, bicycle, and pedestrian access; public transportation routes and stops; bicycle routes; employee and public parking, etc.
- Approved or confirmed changes in vehicular, bicycle, or pedestrian access to your client's building
- Vegetation – identify significant trees or shrubs that, over time, may block important views or vistas or, conversely, become important views or vistas
- Landmarks – man-made or natural
- Views and vistas to and from the site. Important for determining what people see as they approach and leave the building, and for determining end user views (short distances) and vistas (long distances)
- Amenities and services (e.g., retail, restaurants, couriers, etc.)
- Legal information (zoning or land usage)

    Approved or confirmed new structures near the site. These structures could affect sight lines from your client's space, the amount of natural light that enters your client's space, or even acoustics within your client's space

    Photos or video of the site and adjacent areas

Again, in this information collection phase, it doesn't matter how the information is documented. The important thing is that you collect all of the information and document it in some way. With more experience, you might find that having both hard and digital copies of information is useful, particularly when it comes to site plans and architectural drawings. If your client is staying at the same location, having digital copies site plans, roof plans, and other architectural drawings can save you time later on.

Building and Space

The items described in the next paragraph should be recorded when collecting information about your client's existing building and space. Again, if your client is staying in her existing building, you'll want to collect all of the information below. If your client is moving to another building, then you may want to collect just a small amount of information about the existing building such as the main floor plan and photos or video.

If your client's space is within a small building (say, 1–3 stories), you can collect information about the entire building. If your client's space is in a building of more than three stories, it's not necessary to collect information or floor plans for every single floor. Just collect information that has the potential to affect your client's space (i.e., stairs, elevators). Building and space-related information necessary to collect includes:

Floor plan/s. Obtain existing drawings from your client, the local authorities, or the architectural firm. Confirm that the dimensions of the drawings are the same as the built space. If not, jot down on the plans the actual dimensions. If floor plans don't exist, you'll have to sketch them on site, and then draw them up later.

Reflected ceiling plans (RCPs). Again, obtain drawings if possible. RCPs are useful for understanding the ceiling system; lighting; heating, ventilation, and air conditioning (HVAC) system; sprinklers locations; and other ceiling plane information. Understanding the ceiling plane is especially important if the existing ceiling is to remain.

Elevations and/or sections. Sections are preferred because they show plenum spaces and floor assembly thicknesses. Again, if you have existing section drawings, confirm that the drawing and built dimensions are the same. Confirm the accuracy of window heights and door heights.

Photographs and/or video. Record the entire space and potentially important architectural or other details (moldings, staircases, window casings).

Document both positive and negative aspects. A video recording is particularly helpful because you can simultaneously record commentary about the building or space.

Structure. Identify how the building is constructed (e.g., timber frame, pre-cast concrete, steel frame), and identify all load-bearing interior partitions, walls, and columns. The structural system and materials could be important if the eventual designer wants to remove a wall, add stairs, add a second level, or make other modifications that require changes to the building structure. Among other information, the construction method and materials are needed for determining applicable building codes.

Building systems and assemblies. Describe the floor, wall, and ceiling systems. Is the floor a raised floor? Are interior partitions typical drywall? Is the partition framing metal or wood? Is the ceiling exposed, is there suspended ceiling tile with plenum space above, or is the ceiling full drywall?

Mechanical systems. Make general notes about electrical, plumbing, and HVAC systems and equipment. Identify the location of the electrical panel, city water supply, hot water supply, and city sewer. Also, identify location of washrooms and other areas where there is a water supply.

Vertical circulation systems. Note the location of stairs, elevators, lifts, escalators. Note how stairs are constructed (wood, steel, concrete, open rise or closed, etc.). Take pictures of stair details including handrails.

Special systems. Note the location of security equipment or other special systems.

Life safety. Note the location of fire exits, emergency lights, fire extinguishers, etc.

Special characteristics. Does the building have an historical, conservation, or other designation? If so, do you have the proper documents describing what can and cannot be done to the building? If not, track them down. Note any windows, woodwork, staircases, or other architectural features that could possibly be retained or that must be retained.

Furniture inventory. If your client plans to re-use some, or all, of their furniture and equipment, you'll need to create a furniture inventory by taking pictures of each piece, measuring and recording its dimensions counting the number of each piece, and recording any manufacturer information from labels on each piece.

There may be other kinds of information you want to collect about the existing condition. By no means should you limit information collection to the topics described above. Use your best judgement; collect any piece of information that you think might be of value. It is always better to have more information than not enough.

Desired Condition

Shift your thoughts to your client's desired space. From this point on, it's all about the new environment – the one that your client hired you to program. Although you'll be collecting information on the same topics as the existing situation, the amount and kind of information you collect will be quite different. Additionally, you'll need to collect information about the project context.

Context

Familiarizing yourself with, or understanding the context of a project requires investigation into: (a) the project typology, (b) precedents, (c) trends, and (d) the local context. You might be wondering, "Why do I need to collect information on all of these topics?" The answer to this question isn't simple. I'll use a somewhat long scenario to explain why the context of a project is so fundamentally important not only in programming but in design as well.

Let's assume that you've been asked to program the *Extreme Toy Hauler Mobile Showroom* in Appendix C. If you've never had the opportunity to design a showroom, let alone a mobile toy hauler showroom, you'd probably want to start by asking yourself some questions:

- What is a toy hauler?
- What do I know about the toy hauler industry?
- What do I know about showroom design?
- What do I know about mobile showroom design?
- What makes a mobile showroom successful?
- Are there showrooms nearby that I could visit?
- What are the latest trends in showroom design, furniture, equipment, or technology? Are any of these trends research- or evidence-based, and do they need to be?

- What do I know about locations the mobile showroom will travel to?
- What do I know building codes for mobile showrooms or toy haulers?

If you already know the answers to these questions, then you probably don't need to read the rest of this chapter. I'm willing to bet, though, that you don't (I certainly didn't). So, if you examine the questions closely, you'll realize that they are questions about the typology (1–4), precedents (5–6), trends (7), and local context (8–9). You would probably have many other questions as well but most of them would probably fit into one of these four categories. If not, then, by all means, develop additional categories as needed for your particular project.

Finding out about these four things – the typology, precedents, trends, and the local context – will help you develop the broad awareness needed for programming not only a toy hauler mobile showroom, but any project imaginable. Depending on the type of project you're programming, the amount of time available, or your instructor or client's expectations, however, you may not have time to collect information on all four topics. It is quite acceptable to pick and choose which of the four topics you will collect information on. And, again, you may collect information on any topic not included here.

An interior design typology is a type of space that has been designed for a particular purpose, function, or use. Typological investigations are sometimes called "typology studies" or "typological analysis." I like to call them investigations because, at this early phase of the programming process, you are simply collecting information on the typology, not analyzing it.

Interior design typologies exist in two broad categories – residential and commercial (Figure 4.4). Obviously, the function of residential typologies is to house people and all of their "living" activities. Commercial typologies, however, include a wide range of environments for a wide range of activities. Workplace, entertainment, retail, education, healthcare, transportation, hospitality, and spiritual environments are just some of the commercial typologies that exist.

Questions that may guide your typological investigation include: "When did the typology first come into existence?" "How has the typology changed over the years?" "What were some of the defining moments in the evolution of the typology?" "What are some of the physical differences between early and current examples of

	Residential	Single- & multi-family dwellings	Apartments Condominiums	Co-ops
	Institutional	Government Education	Healthcare	
	Healthcare	Hospitals Clinics	Long-term care facilities Dentists, optometrists	
	Workplace	Offices		
	Retail	Boutique Chain stores	Shopping Malls	
	Hospitality	Hotel, motel B & B, hostel	Cafe, restaurant Gaming, casinos	Entertainment
	Cultural	Religious, spiritual Museum, art gallery	Funeral homes	
	Fitness, Sports & Recreation	Arenas Gymnasiums	Health clubs	
	Transportation	Bus, train depots High speed transit	Underground transit stations	Airports Ferry terminals
	Industrial	Manufacturing facilities	Warehouses	

Figure 4.4 Interior design typologies (text by author; icons by istock.com/marvid, and vasabii/stock.adobe.com; illustration by June Bug Design)

the typology?" "How have design concepts, principles, or elements been utilized in the typology?" "What space planning theory is evident in the typology, and how has that theory changed over time?" Answers to these questions will come from design literature.

Simply put, a precedent is a specific example of a typology. Precedents are built interior environments that are similar to the interior environment that you're programming. Precedents can be historical or current. Most students focus on current precedents because current spaces reflect the most up-to-date design thinking. It may be worthwhile, however, to collect information on historical precedents as well. Later, analysis will help you determine whether or not the historical precedents (or the current ones for that matter) are relevant to your project. Whether you use current or historical precedents (or both) depends on the nature of your project.

To demonstrate the difference between typologies and precedents, consider, again, the toy hauler mobile showroom. A typological investigation about showrooms would yield information about a range of showrooms, showroom space planning issues, and perhaps the history of showroom design. A precedent investigation, however, would yield information about one showroom only; a showroom that either exists or has been designed, but not yet built.

Another way to think of a precedent is to think of it as a "best example." What is the best example of a mobile showroom design that you can find? Why is this mobile showroom the best example? Does it incorporate exemplary space planning, lighting, color, or materials? Or, does the precedent have a program similar to your project?

When selecting precedents, it is wise to be aware of the geographic, social, political, and economic context in which the precedent exists. Without awareness of these factors, you could mistakenly assume that a precedent successful in one context would be equally successful in another context.

There are many reasons for choosing a precedent, and ultimately, you'll need to decide what makes your precedent the best choice. A precedent can be selected because it:

- Has won awards
- Has a program similar to your project
- Exemplifies great space planning (zoning, spatial relationships, circulation)
- Exemplifies excellent volumetric design or application of design elements and principles
- Exemplifies superb use of light, color, or materials
- Has unusual elements or design features that are relevant to your project
- Has historical significance
- Is theoretically significant
- Exemplifies a ground-breaking approach

Your instructor may require you, or you may decide on your own, to collect information on more than one precedent. If so, think about selecting each precedent for a different reason. That way, you'll have a wider range of information to analyze later on. In contrast, collecting two or more precedents for the same reason is also valuable because having lots of information on similar precedents may help you identify trends.

When collecting information about precedents, it's always good practice to obtain the following:

- Name of the project
- Address or location
- Owner's name
- The design team (interior designers, architects, engineers, etc.)
- Total ft^2 (m^2)
- Floor plan/s
- Photos
- Written description/s (e.g., magazine article)

Current design magazines are usually a good place to find current precedents but there are other sources as well. One such source is the design firm itself. If you need further information about a precedent that you've seen in a magazine, try sending the design firm an email asking for the needed information.

A colleague of mine, Professor Nancy Maruca, once pointed out that there are at least three kinds of trends – current, emerging, and future trends. Current trends are taking place right now. Emerging trends may happen in the next one-to-five years. Future trends may occur after five years. While current trends are relatively easy to identify, predicting emerging and future trends requires a tremendous amount of knowledge and work. To identify emerging and future trends, large amounts of data must be collected on social, political, economic, and other factors. This information is distilled, and then applied to a particular discipline to speculate about what might be a current, near, or future trend in that discipline.

Interior designers don't have time to do this kind of work. Instead, interior design practitioners follow key publications; news casts; pod casts; social, political, economic trends; real estate trends, and so on to see what trend forecasters are predicting for the future. Practitioners who specialize in a particular type of design (e.g., healthcare, education, retail, hospitality) follow that industry's trends by subscribing to industry-specific publications, web sites, etc. Practitioners then contemplate about how current and emerging trends may affect the way they program, the way they design, or the way they conduct business.

Due to time restrictions, students usually base their programs and designs on existing trends. While this may be acceptable in college or university, in real-life practice, relying solely on current trends could result in a design that is "dated" by the time the space or building is occupied. The reason being, of course, is that real-life projects actually get built. A real-life project could take over five years to complete and, by that time, what was once a trend may now be passé. The lesson here? If you have the time, collect information on both current and emerging trends.

Developing an understanding of the local context in which your real or hypothetical project exists requires investigating the local culture and local, regional, provincial, state, or federal regulations. Collecting information on these topics is particularly important if you aren't familiar with the local context, but equally important even if you are familiar with the context. Sometimes, when we are familiar with a context, we overlook things or assume that we know everything there is to know about the local culture. We can avoid making assumptions by objectively collecting information on the local culture as though we knew nothing about it at all.

One of the first pieces of information you need to collect about a local context is a map showing the project location in relation to its surroundings. If your client is staying in the same location, then you may already have a map, or several maps of the area, collected during the Existing Condition phase. If not, then it's a good idea to collect several maps, at different scales, so that you have a record of the project location in relation to the town, city, district, or borough; the province, state or region; and perhaps even the country.

Coming to understand a local culture means that you need to objectively and subjectively get to know the people, their customs, their architectural design preferences, and maybe even their "quirks." You can collect statistics and census data (objective information) on most neighborhoods or regions, but you can also just watch, mingle, and participate in the local culture (subjective information) to find out more about it. Local newspapers and museums, and conversations with local historians, or local architectural or interior design firms can result in a plethora of information about a particular culture.

Although unusual, you may also collect a three-dimensional object or artifact during the information collection phase. These kinds of objects can be useful not only as reminders of the local culture, but as stimulants for determining project goals or objectives. For example, a special rock, a hand-made craft from a local business or maker, or an item that your client produces (toys, toothbrushes, software) can be used as the starting point for a discussion about the project's main purpose. Goofy? Maybe. But, in design, creative thinking can be stimulated by almost anything.

Local, regional, provincial, state, or federal regulations are particularly important in programming and design. Part of understanding a local context is understanding its life-safety laws, regulations, and standards. You'll want to collect all necessary documents pertaining to building code, accessibility, and other life safety codes and regulations for the area in which your project is located. If you're programming a specific typology such as a healthcare or restaurant environment, collect code information related to that particular industry as well.

For your student project, it may be acceptable to refer to an interior design codebook such as Harmon and Kennon (2014). Their book describes international building and plumbing codes as well as those for the US. Your instructor, however, may require that you use the building and other codes information that apply specifically to your project.

With a broad and rich understanding of the context for your client's desired condition, it is now time to focus on the desired condition specifics. Again, how much and what type of information you collect here will depend on whether or not your client is staying in the same location, whether the desired or new condition will have the same end users as the existing condition, and whether or not your client plans to make changes to their workflow, products they produce or services they supply.

As with the existing condition, you'll want to collect information on people, workflow, products, the site, and the building and space.

People

Three key pieces of people-related information that you need to collect are: (a) your client's goals for the project, (b) assumptions that you and your client have about the project, and (c) the number and type of end users who will use the space. If the desired end users are different than the existing end users, then you will need to collect enough information on the new end users so that you can create the end user profiles that you'll need in phase 3, synthesis.

Project goals are broad, general statements about a design project. Goals usually can't be measured. Your clients may not know what their design goals are, but they probably know what they want the new condition (the new environment) to do for their company, business, or organization. It's your job, as the programmer, to question and probe your clients in order to help them establish design goals. As a programmer, you need project goals so that both you and your client can make effective decisions throughout the programming process. Of course, if your client is an imaginary one, then you can make up project goals as necessary.

The information you've already collected (or imagined and documented) about your client's company, business, or organization is a good starting point for determining project goals. Project goals are varied and there is no single correct way to write them. Nonetheless, goals often center on ideas such as:

Plans for the future. Does the company plan to grow, downsize, or stay the same?

Workflow. Will the company or individual processes remain as they are now, or does your client have any interest in, or need for, changing the way things are done currently?

Products or services. Does your client's company intend to offer the same products or services as they do currently, or will they make changes to those things?

Image or brand identity. What is the image that your client wants to project to her customers, clients, or employees? Is this image or brand in place currently, and if so, does it need to be modified. Does an entirely new image or brand need to be developed?

Function. How does your client see the new environment functioning? Will people in the new space function in pretty much the same fashion as they do currently, or is a new approach needed with regard to how end users function within the space?

Of course, you and your client (or just you) aren't limited to establishing goals related to the topics above. By all means, write any project goal that is appropriate for your particular project.

In the *Blackthorn Live/Create* program (Appendix A), the client's project goals were:

- To have a long-term live/create environment that is flexible and that can be re-configured as her preferences or needs change over time
- To own a building that reflects her values including: freedom, creativity, spontaneity, honesty, and order

In the *Extreme Toy Hauler* (ETH) *Mobile Showroom* program (Appendix C), the clients' project goals were:

- To provide customers with an exceptional retail experience
- To provide employees with an exceptional work experience
- To educate customers about ETH's toy hauler design, innovations, function, and amenities
- To increase the company's profile and generate more sales

Clearly, project goals vary from project to project. But, assuming that your hypothetical project won't be built, it doesn't matter if your goals are perfect. Just try to make them as realistic and reasonable as is possible. Again, the important thing is to identify project goals now, and then stick with them as programming progresses.

Project goals need to drive the program, not the other way around. So, later on if you find yourself frustrated with the direction that your program is taking, don't be tempted to simply change the project goals to suit your program. If you get into the habit of changing goals, objectives, and concepts to suit the program or design, you may be disappointed in real-life practice when clients may not be as agreeable to change things once the program or project is well under way.

In addition to identifying project goals in the information collection phase, it's also important to identify any assumptions that you or your client may have about the desired condition.

Documenting client, programmer, and sometimes end user assumptions is an important programming task that is often over-shadowed by other programming tasks. Unidentified assumptions (whether they're yours, the client's or the end users') can lead to inaccurate programming decisions which, in turn, can lead to inaccurate design solutions.

Another way to think about assumptions is to think of them as biases or preferences. It's easier to ask yourself, "What are my preferences?" than it is to ask, "What are my assumptions?" Topics that programmers and their clients often make assumptions about include style, color, and materials, but assumptions can also be made about workflow, future needs, or even something as simple as your client's hours of operation. Style, color, materials, pattern, texture preferences are easy to identify by using something as simple as a collage. You can create several collages, each with a unique style, and present them to you client as a way of initiating a conversation about preferences. Or, you can simply have a wide range of images and materials on hand from which your client can choose their preferred color, style, pattern, or texture.

The use of collages in programming is not something that I've read about in other programming books. In fact, some designers might think that programmers have no business creating "style" or "image" collages with clients at such an early stage of the design process. As explained here, though, collages are an effective tool for helping you understand your client preferences so that you can program the facility accordingly. Later on in the design process (after programming is complete), the client will have in-depth discussions about style, color, and material preferences directly with the designer.

One last benefit of documenting assumptions is that they can be used later on for evaluating the success of your program. That is, you can compare assumptions to project objectives and design guidelines to see whether you've subconsciously replicated your own preferences rather than met the needs and preferences of your client.

Assumptions established in *The HUB* program (Appendix B) include:

- That the concession will be open all year round
- That an addition will be added to the barn to accommodate mechanical equipment, the bar, and the concession

- That the necessary mechanical, electrical, and plumbing systems will be installed
- That the barn will require structural repairs
- That the entire facility, including the loft, will be accessible

Some of the assumptions in *The HUB* program (Appendix B) may seem obvious, but they're better off documented in order to avoid any misunderstandings that might arise. For example, without stating that the concession will be open all year round, the programmer might assume that since it's a concession stand, it will only be open during the summer. In this case, the client envisions the year-round concession being accessed by customers from both the interior and exterior of the facility.

The final people-related issue that you need to collect information on is, of course, end users. In conversations with your client, or with yourself (if your client is imaginary), you need to determine how many, and what type of end users will use the new environment. Also, if the primary end users in the new condition are going to be different than the existing primary end users then, at this point, you'll need to collect information on the new end users. You'll need this information so that you can generate the end user profiles for draft program document.

For the desired condition end users, you can use the same framework identified earlier in the chapter. That is, you can collect information on:

- Job or position title (or some other classification)
- The type of end user (primary, secondary or tertiary)
- Total number of primary, secondary, and tertiary end users
- Job status (full-time, part-time, contract)
- Number of end users who hold each job title
- End user activities or job responsibilities and tasks
- Frequency and duration of activities
- Degree of visual privacy required
- Degree of acoustic privacy required
- Special and/or future needs
- Gender, age, or other demographic information that could impact programmatic decisions

An important discussion to have with you client about end users is one that focuses on future plans. You may have already had this discussion when you determined project goals but, if not then now is the time to ascertain your client's future plans. If the client's business is expected to expand, when will the expansion take place? Will the desired condition need to accommodate an increased number of end users at some point in the future? Is the future one, two, three, four, or five years down the road? Alternatively, will your client's company downsize in the future? If so, what does your client plan to do with the surplus area in the desired space? As you can imagine, there are many other questions that need to be asked and answered with regard to your client's future plans.

Workflow

Programming can play an important role in terms of workflow because you may discover alternative (and better) ways for your client to conduct his operation or provide services, or for individuals and groups to conduct their day-to-day work. In fact, this is the one area that could have the greatest influence on both the program and the eventual design. Just because your client's company currently operates in a certain way, it doesn't mean that the company must continue to operate the same way in the future.

You should have already collected a document or two that explains your client's existing workflow. A simple conversation with your client (or yourself) will determine whether or not there is any need to revise the company's workflow. If your client is open to suggestions for improved workflow, then you'll need to probe your client about what she thinks are problems with the existing workflow. Chances are that when the company workflow changes, individual workflows will change as well. Whatever the case may be – retain the existing workflow, modify it, or develop an entirely new workflow – ensure that you are clear about the desired condition workflow because this workflow is the one upon which you'll base the majority of your programmatic decisions.

Products

Just like the issue of workflow, you need to have a conversation with your client with regard to the products or services his company provides. Will the company's products or services stay the same, be modified, or change drastically? Will these changes relate to the actual products or services themselves or to the amount of product or quantity of service provided? Will more, or less, space be required to house the company's products? Will more, or less, space be required in order for your company to provide increased services to its customers?

So, again, now is the time to question your client (or decide for yourself) whether or not processes or products will change in the new condition. If the answer is "Yes," then your client needs to provide you with information as to what the new products or services will be.

Recall some of the features of the SPM described in Chapter 3. In that chapter, I wrote that programmers should avoid, or put aside, any pre-conceived ideas about human behavior, spatial form, and spatial or building typology. Also recall the idea that programming can be a catalyst for change. Now is your opportunity. Think outside the box, question your client's workflow, push your client (or yourself) to imagine entirely different ways that his company could operate.

Site

If your client plans to remain in her existing space, then there is little information that you need to collect at this point because you've collected it already. If you were unable to obtain a site plan, site section, or some other drawing while collecting information on the existing space, now is the time to do so. You will need these plans and drawings in the second programming phase, Analysis.

If your client plans to move to a new space in a new or different building on a new site, then you'll need to collect information on the new site, building, and space. And once again, the framework you used earlier to guide information collection on the client's existing site can be used here. A condensed version of the previous framework is as follows:

- Site plan
- Roof plan
- Major streets, rivers, lakes, etc.
- Access to the site
- Approved or confirmed changes regarding access to the site
- Vegetation

- Landmarks
- Views and vistas
- Amenities and services
- Legal information
- Approved or confirmed new structures near the site
- Photos or video of the site and adjacent areas

Building and Space

As with a number of topics in this section, when it comes to the building and the space that your client's business will occupy, you only need to collect new or more information if your client is moving to another building or space. If your client is staying in their current space, then you've probably already collected everything you need. Following is a condensed version of the list described earlier in the chapter:

- Floor plan/s
- Reflected ceiling plans (RCPs)
- Elevations and/or sections
- Photographs and/or video
- Structure
- Building systems and assemblies
- Mechanical systems
- Vertical circulation systems
- Special systems
- Life safety
- Special characteristics
- Furniture inventory

At the end of phase 1, your mind should be saturated with project-related information. You should fully understand your client's existing situation, and your client's goals and expectations for her desired (new) condition. Shortly, you'll begin to make sense of all of this information by analyzing it. Before moving on to the SPM phase 2, however, methods and sources for collecting information are described along with products that result from phase 1.

Collection Methods, Sources, and Products

The student programming model (SPM) includes numerous methods for information collection and analysis as well as a few for synthesis, evaluation, and communication. As you gain confidence and experience in programming, you may wish to develop, or use, methods beyond those explained in this chapter and in upcoming chapters. Doing so is not only acceptable, it is desirable. Recent publications on evidence- and research-based programming and design (Botti-Salitsky, 2009; Dickinson and Marsden, 2009; Nussbaumer, 2009) are excellent sources for furthering your knowledge about programming methods whether they be information collection, analysis, or other methods.

In programming courses that I've taught, students almost always ask: "How much information should I collect?" I always respond with, "Collect as much information as you can within the timeframe you have," and, "You want enough information to be able to make trustworthy and valid decisions." The reason I respond this way, is that the more evidence you have (especially if it's from a wide variety of sources), the more likely it is that your clients, instructors, and peers will believe in, and trust your programmatic decisions. If your program is based on evidence from only one magazine article and a few photocopies from a book, then your client or instructor will be suspicious about the reliability of your program. If you base a program on evidence from a variety of sources including magazine articles, site visits, journals, books, interviews and observation, then your client or instructor will be much more confident that your program document is reliable.

Collection Methods

Four methods can be used for gathering programmatic information: reading, interviewing, observing, and recording. Early on, I included a fifth method – surveys – but soon realized that students would rarely, if ever, have the time or resources to conduct a proper survey. If you wish to use surveys to collect information, you can consult any one of many books devoted to the subject.

When thinking about how best to explain the four information collection methods, I concluded that I had two options; one, explain the methods using research language (and scare you away) or two, explain the methods in a way that interior designers will appreciate. I chose the latter; not just because this book is for interior design students and not because interior designers can't understand research methods, but because there are plenty of books available on research methods, and there are fewer available on research methods for interior design programmers.

Students aiming to earn a professional interior design degree (that enables them to become certified and practice interior design) spend most of their time and energy on design rather than research. As such, the information gathering methods they're most likely to use for programming are ones that will yield the greatest amount of credible information in the shortest amount of time. It is in this spirit that the information gathering methods are described.

I'm willing to bet that you've gathered many documents throughout your academic career, and that you're more than familiar with how to get the documents you need. But, as it turns out gathering relevant documents in an efficient manner for programming does require a bit of planning. Productive document gathering begins with asking yourself a few questions. What information do you need to collect? Where are you most likely to find this information? What information sources are available to you? How much time you have to gather the information? Without thinking about these questions and carefully planning your document-gathering excursion, you risk wasting time by having to backtrack to obtain missing or important information, or running out of time to collect the information you need.

Up to this point in your life, I am also willing to bet that you've done a lot of reading. As a programmer, you may (or may not) be happy to know that you're going to have to continue doing a lot of reading. There is much to learn about the entire project context, and about your client's existing and desired situations. The more you read, the deeper will be your understanding about the project. If you just like to skim over the details, you're probably going to miss critical information that could impact the quality of your program.

It's best to read documents without a highlighter in your hand. Leave the highlighting until the analysis phase. Instead, simply read the documents you collect and write a brief summary about each one that describes its main point or potential value. If you're going to write the summaries on sticky notes, be sure that they are really sticky because once the documents begin to pile up, it may be difficult to know which document a runaway sticky belongs to. It is also a good idea to start putting the documents into piles – existing condition and desired condition piles at the very least. Refer back to the beginning of this chapter if you need a reminder about getting organized.

Perhaps reading doesn't seem like much of an information gathering method to you, but careful reading will help you select quality information that will be useful for programming rather than collecting heaps of information that may or may not be useful for programming. Information gathering isn't about quantity, it's about quality so read a lot and read carefully. Be selective about information that you put in your binder or digital files. Information that you think maybe isn't really all that pertinent can be kept in a separate pile.

When collecting information related to the desired condition context (typology, precedent, trends, local context), I can imagine you doing interviews with designers of spaces similar to the one you're programming, experts in a discipline like the one your client or end users belong to (e.g., nurse practitioners if your program is for a clinic or hospital), or trend forecasters if you have access to them. Just like formal research, the reason for conducting these interviews is to obtain first-hand accounts about a particular topic, industry, discipline, or design issue. Unlike formal research, however, the primary, or raw, data that you collect will not be analyzed according to very strict rules associated with the interview research methodology.

Interviews are conducted in order to gain insight that can't be obtained using other information collection methods. Even for hypothetical projects, you may want to interview a variety of people in order to get that missing piece of information needed to help you understand the whole project context. If you have a real client, you most certainly will want to interview her, probably more than once, about her company's existing and desired situations. If you have a real client, she may be able to provide access to an employee who might have valuable information concerning the existing or desired condition.

Whether or not you interview people for your project depends on how much time you have, how valuable you think the potential information will be, whether or not you have real clients, or your instructor's expectations.

For interior design practitioners, interviewing is the most common method of information gathering used. This is because practitioners have a lot of meetings with their clients – and other individuals – throughout the duration of a project. And even though practitioners don't think of these encounters as anything more than meetings, in reality, these meetings are a type of informal or open-ended interview.

Seasoned practitioners are good at facilitating meetings because they've had lots of practice. If you've never led a meeting or conducted an interview, though, some things to keep in mind include:

- Have a list of questions prepared in advance
- Be prepared to listen. Interviewees are sometimes annoyed or put off if the interviewer dominates the conversation. If this happens, interviewees can "shut down" or clam up because they feel that you're not really interested in their responses
- Be prepared to let the conversation flow naturally. This may mean that your list of questions will be answered in a different order than you planned, but if you want the interviewee to feel relaxed and comfortable, then you need to act relaxed and comfortable yourself. You can't exhibit signs of anxiety about your list of questions or anything else
- Don't use slang or jargon. Keep your vocabulary simple
- Keep the questions simple and to the point
- Have a list of probes on hand in the event that your interviewee needs to be prompted to answer the initial question, or to use when you want the interviewee to expand on one of their responses
- Ask, ahead of time, if you can record the conversation. That way you can focus on the conversation rather than on note-taking
- Be prepared to meet the interviewee where and when it's convenient for them

It is always a good idea to transcribe the interview once it's complete. Transcribing is simply the process of transferring the recorded audio into a text format. Although transcribing is a simple process, it is intensive and expensive. Although people can be hired to compete this task, you probably don't have the time or money to do so. So, what do you do?

It is not always necessary to transcribe an entire interview word-for-word because, again, you're not going to analyze the data using the same stringent rules as those required in research. Maybe after listening to the recording a few times, you can simply jot down the key points.

Interior designers and programmers are inherently observant. Observation is a skill that you're taught very early on in your design education, and is one that you hone as you go through your design education. As is the case with interviews, there is a difference between observation done for design programming purposes and observation done for research. The difference is related to how data is collected and analyzed.

Observation can be used to gather information about your client's existing and desired conditions. In terms of context, I can imagine you observing conditions while on a site visit to a building or space similar to the one you're programming, observing human activities or spatial characteristics in your client's existing space, or observing site, building and space conditions at your client's desired site. As a programmer, you are most likely to make notes about, take photos of, or video record whatever it is that you observe.

Using observation while on site visits (to your client's facility or similar facilities) is an extremely valuable method for learning about your client's workflow and about end user behavior and interaction in your client's facility and in similar facilities. Observing behavior, especially if people are unaware that they are being observed, provides tremendous insight into how really people spend their time. In an interview, for example, a person might tell you that they spend x amount of time doing this or that. Through observation, however, you may discover that what that person told you does not seem to be entirely true. If this occurs, you may be tempted to jump to the conclusion that the person you interviewed and observed is less than truthful. Suspend this thought. Good observers focus on recording what they see rather than on making judgements about what they see. Again, you can leave any speculation until the analysis phase.

Like most of the other information gathering methods, site visits require planning prior to conducting the visit. Usually, you will have established a contact person, introduced yourself, explained the purpose for the visit, and stated the expected amount of time that the visit should take. It is critical to determine, ahead of the visit, what information you need to collect. Are you interested in how the facility operates or how it looks and functions (design)? Are you interested in building systems (structural, mechanical, plumbing), or building technologies (security systems, etc.)? Is there a particular feature that you want to understand, or are you just wanting to get an overall sense of the place? Do you need to take measurements, photographs, or video of the facility? Do you have permission to take photos, etc.? Will you need to draw or sketch any diagrams?

The amount and type of information that can be collected while on a site visit is almost endless, but you don't need to collect every single piece of information possible. You would be on the site for days if that was your objective. Just focus on observing information related to your client's existing or desired condition.

In addition to preparing a list of things that you want to observe on site, it is always a good idea to bring along a pad of paper, a measuring tape or app, a pencil, and your smart phone or tablet with camera and video capabilities. With the appropriate apps, you can measure and record almost everything you need to right on your phone or tablet. Also, think about how you might collect the information while on site. If someone is going to be guiding you through a facility and explaining things as you proceed, it might be a good idea to bring along a friend or classmate who can record notes, take photos, etc. while you engage with your tour guide.

Finally, if you plan to visit more than one site (not including your client's existing or new site), is your intent to compare the two or more sites? If so, what criteria will you be comparing? It is best to determine these criteria ahead of time so that you don't forget to collect all of the necessary information while on site. The last thing you want to do on any site visit is forget to document a critical piece of information. This is especially true if you've travelled a fair distance to get to the site. Of course, it may be possible to obtain the information from your site contact person, but avoid doing this if you can.

Once again, I'm sure that you're already an expert at recording information because you've been doing it most of your life. Obviously, you've word processed or written notes by hand, you've drawn pictures, and you've taken photos or video of people or things. These are the typical ways that people, not just programmers, record or document information. So what advice could I possibly offer that would help you record programmatic information efficiently and effectively? Probably not much other than the obvious but I'll offer it anyway.

First, when recording visual information through drawing or photos, it's important to keep track of what it is that you're recording. On drawings, it's easy to write a view notes that describe the context of the image that you just drew. With digital photos, however, there is no way of recording what each picture is without taking the picture, loading it to your image software program, and giving it a name. To stay organized, you would have to do this while on site and it would take forever. We all know the agony of having a ton of images but forgetting, or not being able to figure out, where the images were taken, or even what the images were of.

I'm sure there will be "an app for that" one day, but in the meantime, one solution to keeping digital photos organized is to take photos in a certain order. For instance, you can take photos of all doors and windows first, then take a few photos with your finger in front of the lens so that you have a few "imageless images" that act as a queue for when you're switching to another type of image. Next, you might record the entire ceiling plane or maybe just lighting. Again, leave two or three blank images and then photograph the next item of interest. This is a rather primitive method but at least you'll have an organized set of photos to work with, and won't have to spend hours sorting out the images once you get back to your workspace.

A more complex way of keeping your photographs organized is to use a floor plan to document where each photo, or group of photos, is taken. On the plan, you can indicate how many photos you took from each particular point, and the direction you were aiming at when you took the photos. The floor plan can quickly become cluttered, so you'll probably want to practice this technique a few times before relying on it.

Keeping video recordings organized is much simpler than keeping digital photos organized because, of course, you can use your voice to describe what it is you're recording. The other benefit of video recording is that you can get a better sense of what it's like to move through a space and this can lead to an overall better understanding of the space. If you have a limited time to record information, video is the best choice because still shots can be extracted from the video later.

Finally, recording by hand drawing. With all of the technology and apps that exist today, I probably can't convince you that hand drawing is an important and valuable recording method, but hand drawing does have it benefits. For instance, if your phone or tablet battery is dead while you are on site and you need to record information, you can resort to good old hand drawing. Or, because hand drawing has the potential to capture the essence of something much better than a digital photo or video, hand drawing might be the best choice for recording certain information.

Out of the four information collection methods described above, the two that you'll use most often are reading and recording. You might use interviews occasionally, but you'll be less likely to use observation. The reason reading and recording are used most frequently is simply the lack of time students have to use other methods. Student projects usually have tight timelines – not unlike practice – except that, in college and university, there is just one person doing all of the work – you.

The information gathering methods that you choose to use is up to you. Select ones that will yield the widest and deepest amount of information possible in the time that you have available.

Collection Sources

Three things are important when considering information sources: credibility, publication date, and breadth and depth.

Credible information is published by recognized individuals or authors from credible institutions, associations, governments, and other organizations. Credible information may be found on the internet but care must be taken when using such information. What makes information credible is the qualifications, expertise, experience, education, or peer-recognition of the author or authors who wrote the information. Today, with the availability of information on the internet, it is quite easy to check someone's professional background and qualifications by doing a simple name search, but it's equally easy to assume that if it's on the internet, it must be credible. Don't fall into that trap. People can make themselves look credible by creating official-looking websites for official looking businesses. Do your due diligence and investigate each source. If known credible authors haven't cited a source that you're considering using, then your source is either not credible, or has not made any significant contributions to her field. If you can't find much information about the author of a document or publication you want to use, then don't bother collecting the document and find another source instead.

Your second concern, when collecting information, should be the publication date of the material. Usually, you'll collect the most recent information available; however, there are times when you need to include information published a while back. How far back into history you go depends on how much time you have available to collect information, and on the relevancy of that information to your particular programming assignment. For example, if your programming project relates to an historic facility or time period, then older literature may be more useful to you than current literature.

Sometimes, collecting publications ranging from older to newer, or vice versa, is helpful for understanding timelines, evolutions, typologies, theories, contexts, or other things that have changed over time. Additionally, older publications are sometimes the foundation upon which newer publications are based. As such, you may need to refer to the original publication in order to confirm recent interpretations of the original idea. Don't believe everything you read, especially paraphrases or quotes. Always go to the original source to confirm.

Breadth and depth of information should be your third concern in terms of sources. Breadth and depth can help you establish validity or trustworthiness for your program decisions and final program document; but, in and of itself, a wide range of high quality (not superficial) information will not establish validity. You'll need to analyze the information thoroughly in order for it to make sense, and in order to be able to apply it to your program. In other words, it isn't enough to just collect good information, you need to do something with that information in order to maximize its usefulness.

Keep in mind that not all of the books, magazines, journals, or other sources of information you collect will come from, or need to come from, the design disciplines. In fact, it is best to gather a combination of information from design and other disciplines including that of your client. Multi-disciplinary information will contribute to a deeper understanding of the project context than it will be if you collect information from design sources only.

And finally, the actual sources of information. As shown the lists provided just before the summary, programmatic information can come from a wide variety of people, things, or places. Despite the long list of potential sources, you only need to use the ones that make sense for your project.

Collection Products

Like information sources, there are many products that can result from phase 1 (Table 4.1). Again, it's not necessary, nor desirable to collect all of these products. Just collect products that make sense for your project. By far, most of the information you collect will consist of documents, but you should end up with a significant number of photos, maps, site plans, and architectural drawings as well. If you took my advice from the beginning of this chapter, all of this information will be contained in a well-organized binder or in a set of digital file folders.

Topics	Methods	Sources	Products
Existing condition	Read	People	Building code, accessibility, life safety regulations
People	Interview	Client	Demographic information
Workflow	Observe	End-users	Transcripts
Products	Record	Your client's employees	Brochures, pamphlets related to your client's business
Site		Your client's customers or clients	Description of your client's business
Building/space		Land owners	Organizational charts
Desired condition		Building owners	Affinity diagrams
Context		Architects, engineers, interior designers (of your clients existing space, and new space)	Sociograms
Typology		Locals	End user profiles
Precedent		Experts in a particular field (e.g., healthcare)	Architectural drawings, sketches
Trends		Forecasters	Site, building, space descriptions
Local context		**Places**	Site maps, local area maps
Project		Library, archives, museums	Furniture inventory
People		Businesses, industries, companies, or organizations related to design, design products, or to your client's industry	Photos, videos
Workflow		Governments	Physical artifacts, souvenirs, or mementos
Products		Building sites and adjacent areas	
Site		Similar projects (site visits)	

Topics	Methods	Sources	Products
Building and space		**Things**	
		Books	
		Journals, magazines, newspapers, mirofiche, pamphlets, brochures, reports, employee records	
		Design discipline or other disciplines	
		Databases	
		Websites, blogs, forums, podcasts, TED talks, social media	
		Built environments	
		Natural environments	

Summary

The ever important first phase of the SPM was the focus of this chapter. For some of you, this chapter may have been a bit overwhelming. If it was, then you've understood the importance of collecting programmatic information. You've grasped the idea that becoming saturated with information is exactly what programmers need to do in this first programming phase.

To summarize, you can use four methods for collecting information: (a) reading, (b) interviewing, (c) observing, and (d) recording. You can use these methods to collect information on your client's existing and desired conditions, and the information you collect will come from a variety of sources including: (a) people, (b) places, and (c) things. The products that result from the SPM collection phase vary but usually include documents, photos, maps, and architectural drawings.

If you've collected information in a systematic way, managed to stay organized throughout the process, and obtained all of the information you need, then you've successfully completed phase 1. Congratulations.

References

Botti-Salitsky, Rose Mary. 2009. *Programming and Research: Skills and Techniques for Interior Designers.* New York: Fairchild.

Dickinson, Joan, and John P. Marsden, eds. 2009. *Informing Design*. New York: Fairchild.

Harmon, Sharon K. and Katherine E. Kennon. 2014. *The Codes Guidebook for Interiors*. 6th ed. Hoboken, NJ: Wiley.

Hershberger, Robert G. 1999. *Architectural Programming and Predesign Manager*. New York: McGraw-Hill.

Nussbaumer, Linda L. 2009. *Evidence-based Design for Interior Designers*. New York: Fairchild.

Chapter 5

ANALYSIS

I wish that the analysis phase was just a nice little place in the programming process where you could pause and calmly reflect on the information you've collected so far, and on the project as a whole; unfortunately, it is not. Analysis is one of those deep, dark areas where most people, not just students, don't want to go. This is because there is no quick and simple way to get through analysis. For your program to be successful, you'll need to spend a significant amount of time poring over information to find ideas, issues, themes, or connections that, at first glance, are not apparent. Your hard work will be rewarded, though, with an abundance of ideas, options, possibilities, and ultimately, a deep understanding of your programming project.

Overview

Like most students, you probably find the task of analysis somewhat mystifying. What exactly does analysis mean, and more importantly, how do you go about doing it? To analyze something means to take it apart – to dissect it – in order to fully understand it, and to understand how it (the analyzed thing) fits with other things and with the whole. In research, analysis is done using statistics, content analysis, and grounded theory, to name a few methods. In design, analysis is done using less formal, but just as effective, methods.

In programming, you'll use analysis methods appropriate for helping you reach your long-term objective – a program document that describes your client's desired condition. Five simple methods for analyzing programmatic information include: (a) dissect (text), (b) crunch (numbers), (c) assess, (d) annotate, and (e) draw. You'll use these methods to identify four things: (a) themes, (b) options, (c) project objectives, and (e) design guidelines. All of this may sound easy enough, but analysis is actually a complex process. While in the throes of analysis, you'll find your mind turning in different directions all at once, and you'll find that your hands are barely able to keep up with documenting the abundance of ideas practically falling out of your head. At least, that's been my experience. Analysis is exhilarating; it gets your blood flowing.

Perhaps the most crucial thing about analysis is that you focus your attention on the desired condition, not the existing condition. This doesn't mean that you ignore all of the information you collected regarding your client's existing condition. In fact, if your client's company is staying in the same building and space, then a lot of the information that you'll use in analysis will come from the existing condition information you collected. Alternatively, if your client is moving to another site, building, and space, then you'll analyze the information you collected about your client's desired condition. Even in this situation, though, it's beneficial to review existing condition information every so often to ensure that you're not simply replicating conditions that your client already has. While you're at it, the analysis phase is a good time to review the assumptions identified in phase 1, again, to ensure that you're not subconsciously programming with your own preferences in mind rather than your client's.

So, what exactly is it that you are supposed to analyze? The answer – the information collected in phase 1. Now is the time to do something with all of that precious information that you collected. In this phase, you'll analyze information concerning the desired condition including the project context (typology, precedents, trends, local issues) people, workflow, products, site, and the building and space.

In a nutshell, analysis is about using the information you collected in phase 1 to figure out what the desired condition should be; what the eventual interior environment needs to have in it, how the new environment should function, how activity

Table 5.1 Holding tank form (by author)

		Categories			
		Themes	**Options**	**Project objectives**	**Design guidelines**
Desired condition topics	Site				
	Building and space				
	Workflow				
	Number of end users				
	End user activities				
	Activity zone requirements				
	Area requirements				
	Spatial adjacencies				
	Zoning				
	Circulation				

areas need to be arranged within the new space, and so on. Yes, you've collected information about the desired condition, but without analysis, that information is pretty much useless.

Analysis is where options are generated, considered, compared, and assessed; where programs that are catalysts for change are conceived; and where you consider every possibility, take nothing for granted, and assume nothing. Analysis is the heart of the program; without it, you'll have to magically transform all of that information from phase 1 into a final program. Good luck with that.

Table 5.1 is a simple form that can be used to keep track of emerging themes, options, project objectives, and design guidelines; the four key things that you want, and need, to result from your analysis efforts. I call this form the "holding tank" because it's a "one-stop-shop" where you can keep track of all of your most important ideas. The form is useful for keeping organized and reducing the frustration that can arise during analysis. Obviously, to be useful, you'll have to enlarge the form, or make your own form, and print it on a tabloid (A3) piece of paper.

The categories and topics included on the holding tank form provide a framework to keep you focused throughout the analysis phase. As mentioned earlier, the four main categories across the top row include themes, options, design objectives, and design guidelines. Along the far-left column are topics concerning your client's desired condition; ones that, by now, you should be familiar with. These include: (a) site, (b) building and space, (c) workflow, (d) number of end users, (e) end user activities, (f) activity zone requirements, (g) area requirements, (h) spatial adjacencies, (i) zoning, and (j) circulation. Identifying themes and options related to these ten topics provides you with a starting point for your analysis journey.

Two pieces of advice with regard to using the holding tank… One, don't limit your analysis to the topics or categories on the holding tank form; if there are other topics that need to be explored through analysis, then, by all means, do so. Two, don't feel as though you need to fill in every single box on the form. Identify themes if they emerge naturally; identify options if they emerge naturally. Try not to force themes, options, objectives, or guidelines.

Themes

Finding themes among similar types of information is relatively easy but can be time-consuming. Themes occur when a pattern is established through repetition. In order to identify patterns, you need to spend significant time reading, and re-reading the information you collected in phase 1.

A theme's strength can be measured by the number of times the theme (or topic) arises, and by the variety of information sources from which the theme arises. For instance, a theme can be considered "strong" or significant when you have, say, five out of eight pieces of information all pointing toward the same theme. The theme might be considered even more significant if the five pieces of information are from very different sources.

For example, in the Extreme Toy Hauler program (Appendix C), themes emerged about augmented reality (AR) being used to sell automobiles, and about immersive and experiential retail experiences. Had it not been for analysis, these themes aren't ones that I would have identified at first glance. More importantly, these themes are ones that eventually became important project objectives; objectives that became the heart of the final program. As is evident in this example, what you may identify as a theme on the holding tank form can eventually become a project objective. There are times when themes can become design guidelines as well. There is no rule to say that once you place an idea in a certain column, it must remain there.

Themes can emerge by finding connections between different amounts or types of information. Again, in the Extreme Toy Hauler program, I was able to make connections between automobile showrooms, the retail industry in general, mobile showrooms, and toy haulers. This happened because I couldn't find any precedents or typological information on toy hauler showrooms specifically. But, by making connections between themes from these somewhat diverse contexts (automobile and retail industries, and showroom precedents), I was able to make important connections that strongly influenced the design program.

As noted in Chapter 4, the amount of information you collect for a programming project depends on a number of variables: (a) how much time you have to collect information, (b) the amount of information readily available, and (c) your client or instructor's expectations. So, when it comes to identifying themes, it may well be that you have very limited information on your topic. If that's the case, don't try to force them (themes). Forced themes will be inaccurate and may lead you to make incorrect or poor programming decisions. Instead, go back to phase 1 and collect more information. Although this probably isn't the solution you expected, or wanted to hear, realistically it is the only solution that will result in an objective, evidence-based design program.

In most cases, if you have a good amount and variety of information, spend enough time with your information, and are rigorous enough, themes are likely to emerge on their own. In addition to design-related themes, you may find some that relate to your client's business or to societal, political, or economic trends that could impact your program. Don't ignore these; jot them down on the holding tank form. You can always discard unimportant themes later on.

A rigorous method for identifying themes is called "content analysis," and my version of it – dissecting text – is described shortly.

Options

Using a variety of analysis methods to generate options is a way of transforming alpha-numeric information into what will eventually become three-dimensional form. Options are a crucial part of analysis because they enable you to realize all of the possibilities for your client's desired condition before having to make decisions about, or having to choose, the best options.

In programming interior environments, analysis always involves generating options for spatial issues such as area calculations, spatial relationships, and circulation. However, if your client wants to change her organization's workflow, then you'll need to generate options for enabling the company to become more efficient in its processes, or change the way people, information, and products move through the client's space. So, whether you're generating standard spatial options, or options for unique issues or situations, well-analyzed options will provide you with a good variety of choices that you'll need when you set out to create the draft program in phase 3, synthesis.

As you'll see shortly, options can be generated using lists, tables, schematic drawings, or freehand sketches. What's important to note here, is that when you generate any kind of option, you need to record your thoughts about, or rationale for, each option. Without recording these thoughts, the options may end up being meaningless to you later on because you will have forgotten what the option was for or why you generated the option in the first place. Annotation is a quick and easy way to record your thoughts, and it's an analysis method that's described later in the chapter.

By the end of the chapter, you'll understand how themes and options can help you generate project objectives, and how project objectives can be ranked to determine priorities. These ranked priorities will serve as the starting point for phase 3, synthesis.

Project Objectives

Project objectives will emerge as you trudge through the analysis quagmire. They might emerge while dissecting text, crunching numbers, or combining information from two diverse topics or sources. How they emerge is not as important as is recognizing them when they do emerge. So, what are they? Well, they're different than the project goals that you and your client fabricated during the information collection phase. Those goals were broad and mostly unmeasurable. Project objectives are mostly measurable outcomes of the eventual design project. They are the essence of the finished design. They capture and describe the things that make your project different from other projects.

When you have real clients, identifying project objectives is easier than when you're trying to fabricate them yourself. Nonetheless, if you are really committed to your project, are truly saturated with project information, and are thoroughly prepared to spend significant time engaging in analysis, then I'm absolutely positive that at least a few project objectives will emerge. In college and university, you can discuss emerging objectives with your peers or instructors to ensure that each one is unique and appropriate for your project.

Project objectives often relate to the function, aesthetic, or essence of the eventual interior environment. They are specific to each project, and each objective is unique. Objectives such as sustainability, accessibility, circulation, or lighting are not appropriate objectives because they apply to almost all projects. That is, they are not unique; all well-designed interiors should address sustainability, accessibility, circulation, and lighting (among other things). That said, if there is something unique or special about any one of these things, then these topics may, in fact, be developed into appropriate objectives.

Project objectives must be specific to the project you are programming. At the same time, they need to be broad enough to allow the eventual designer a reasonable degree of creativity in terms of how the objectives might be met. If the objectives are generic, chances are the end result will be generic. If the objectives are too specific, the designer may feel "hemmed in," and unable to generate creative solutions.

In the *Blackthorn Live/Create* program (Appendix A), project objectives included:

- Creating an environment of contrasts that reflects Kate's character
- Creating a flexible environment that can be altered with little effort
- Designing four visually and acoustically separate areas; one for living, one for digital graphic art work, one for airbrush work, and one for personal reflection
- Providing a secure environment for Kate's pricey investments, including her graphic design and airbrush equipment, as well as her vintage scooter collection

The number of project objectives you develop will vary from project to project; anywhere between three and five is usually adequate. Too many objectives can lead to conflict. If you do happen to have a long list of objectives, you'll need to prioritize them and choose maybe the top 3–5. If necessary, remove some objectives from the list, or establish a list of secondary objectives.

In projects where you don't have a real client, the important thing to keep in mind – as the programming process proceeds – is that you stick to the project objectives that you establish. In the Evaluation and Revision phase, you'll have an opportunity to modify project objectives or identify new priorities, and later on, I'll explain why.

Design Guidelines

Design guidelines are included in this chapter because it's through analysis that they begin to take shape. These guidelines consist of three parts; issues, objectives, and concepts but it's only the issues that you'll identify in analysis. You'll use the identified issues later, in synthesis, to formulate the full design guidelines. So, what are they?

Design guidelines are sort of like a summary of the program. They highlight important design issues that the eventual designer will need to address. Like project objectives, design guidelines should not be generic; both should be unique. Design guidelines are the things that distinguish your project from others. Given the similarity between project objectives and design guidelines – at least in terms of intent – it is sometimes hard to distinguish between them. This, you'll be delighted to know, is a good thing, because it means that you'll probably have fewer revisions to do in the next programming phase.

What distinguishes objectives from guidelines is that guidelines are more specific; they are written for designers in order to guide, or "steer" designers in the direction that you think your client wants to go. And, what distinguishes objectives from project goals (as noted earlier), is that objectives are more specific and measurable than goals. As you can see then, the difference between goals, objectives, and guidelines is the degree of specificity in each of them. Goals are broad, objectives are focused, and guidelines are specific.

The phrase "design guidelines" is not one that I have seen in other programming models or texts, but it's one that I use to describe what is, essentially, the design program summary. I use a specific structure and format for design guidelines but it's not one that I developed on my own. Robert Kumlin (1995) developed the structure that I use, only he calls it a theoretical framework for architectural programming.

In his framework, Kumlin (1995) uses the word "issue" to describe generic concerns that clients provide to architectural programmers. Then, he uses the word "objective" to explain potential ways that each issue could be addressed. Finally, he uses the word "concept" to describe potential solutions or ways that each objective could be met. Kumlin's framework is a beautiful one because it's simple, effective, and doesn't make the architect feel like she "must do this," or "must do that." In fact, Kumlin emphasizes, quite heavily, the idea that objectives and concepts must always be posed speculatively rather than concretely.

Further explanation about design guidelines is explained in phase 3, synthesis. For now, this brief explanation is all you need in order to understand why design guideline issues here should be identified here in analysis, and recorded here on the holding tank form.

Time to move onto the methods – the techniques you'll use to analyze your information and generate all of the themes, options, project objectives, and design guidelines need for the looming third phase, synthesis.

Analysis Methods

Early drafts of this chapter included a long list of analysis methods from the social sciences and design disciplines. It wasn't until much later in the writing process when I realized that there are really only five methods that interior design programmers need to use. These simple but powerful methods require programmers to: (a) dissect (text), (b) crunch (numbers), (c) assess, (d) annotate, and (e) sketch. That's it. Nothing fancy, nothing overly complex. Just five straight forward techniques for making sense out of the information you collected in phase 1. Yes, many more methods of analysis exist, but for me, analyzing programmatic information doesn't require special skills beyond common sense, the ability to think, and the ability to do basic math.

Dissect (Text)

Dissecting text is a somewhat cheeky phrase for what researchers call "content analysis." Content analysis is a systematic process used to identify themes within

Table 5.2 Content analysis form (by author)

1st read themes	1st read theme descriptions	Edited themes	Edited theme descriptions	Code	Frequency	Frequency total	Rank

text-based information. This type of analysis requires reading through, and coding all of the information you've collected. It is a laborious process because it requires at least five "reads" of all of your information in order to identify themes that accurately reflect the content you're analyzing. In programming, content analysis is useful for analyzing precedents, theories, trends, historical information, and evidence.

Using content analysis requires patience and tenacity. Often, students are in too much of a hurry to undertake this kind of analysis. For those of you up to the challenge, though, content analysis can yield rewarding results – themes that may not have been obvious at first glance. Table 5.2 is a form that is quite useful for keeping track of emerging themes during content analysis. As with the holding tank form, you'll need to enlarge the Content Analysis form and print it on a tabloid (A3) sheet in order to have the space necessary to write down your findings.

The process for conducting content analysis goes something like this:

1. Assemble all of the information that you want to include in the analysis. Make photocopies of all of the information, because content analysis is a messy process that leaves you with heavily marked up documents that are difficult to read. It may be wise to enlarge your photocopies so that you have plenty of room for coding (step six explains what coding entails).

Given the wide range of information you've collected, it's quite possible that not all information you have will be suitable for content analysis. For instance, building code information, employee records, and site plans; these types of information aren't usually suitable for content analysis.

2. Once you've decided which information to analyze, take each document one-by-one and read it. As you read, use a pencil to underline words, phrases, or sentences that you think are important given the context of your program.

   In very stringent content analysis, you would select a "unit of analysis" before starting. The unit of analysis could be a word, phrase, sentence, or paragraph. In your analysis, you underline only words, phrases, sentences, or paragraphs—whichever unit of analysis you selected. For programming, I find that using a single unit of analysis is too restricting, and that's is why I recommend underlining anything that you think is important whether it be a word, phrase, or sentence.

3. In your second read of the information, check to make sure that you've underlined all of the important information. If there's something you missed, underline it now.

4. During the third read of information, you'll begin to identify themes. As you read the first underlined word, phrase, or sentence, decide on a word or short phrase that captures the main idea of the underlined content. Write this word or phrase in column one of Table 5.2, and write down a brief description of each theme in column two. Continue to do this until you reach the end of your document, and then repeat the process for every other document that you want to analyze.

   As you begin to assign names to emerging themes, I recommend using a technique called, "constant comparison." This technique, borrowed from qualitative research methods, requires you to constantly compare information to determine if the information is the same, similar, or different than previous information. So, rather than creating a new theme for every single piece of information that you've underlined, compare the word, sentence, or phrase that you are analyzing to already-established themes to see if the new information could belong to one of those categories. If not, then by all means, create a new theme.

   After reading all of your information and establishing preliminary themes, assess the themes you've established. You may notice similarities between themes and decide to "collapse" two or more themes into one. Likewise, if some themes are too broad, break them down into two or more themes. In these situations, you'll want to create revised theme names and descriptions to better reflect the amalgamated or separated themes. If you've revised the themes and/or descriptions, write them in columns three and four in Table 5.2.

5. Once you are satisfied with your list of themes and their descriptions, give each theme a "code," which is essentially a unique symbol or identifier. This identifier could be a number, single letter, group of letters, or some other symbol. Whatever code or symbol you choose, write it down in column five of Table 5.2. In your fourth reading of the information, you will use these symbols to code the underlined information.

6. In the fourth read, code each underlined word, phrase, or sentence by putting the appropriate symbol beside it. I usually put these codes at the beginning of each word, phrase, or sentence rather than at the end but it doesn't really matter where you put the code as long as you're consistent. Continue to code all of the important information until you've coded all of your documents.

7. In your fifth reading, put a tick mark beside each code every time you come across it. This will ensure that you've accounted for every coded piece of information. Immediately after you tick each coded word, phrase, or sentence in the document, put a tick mark in the appropriate row of column six (Table 5.2). Do this with all of your information.

8. In column six, count the tick marks beside each theme and write down the total in column seven. Now you'll know which themes occurred more frequently than others. The higher the frequency, the stronger the theme.

9. In column eight, list the themes in order of frequency with the highest frequency being number one. Transfer this ranked list of themes to your holding tank master sheet (Table 5.1).

If you're put off by, or don't have enough time to complete the full content analysis method, you can always do a slightly abbreviated version of it. In the abbreviated version, you simply eliminate steps 1, 3, and 8.

Crunch (Numbers)

Crunching numbers, or analyzing numeric information, is something that programmers do a lot of during the Analysis phase. If you're not particularly "good at math," don't worry. In programming, number crunching involves basic skills such as addition and subtraction.

Although most number crunching methods are rather simple, you shouldn't under-estimate their usefulness as analysis tools. As demonstrated in the dissect text, or content analysis, method, counting the frequency with which something occurs is a simple way of demonstrating the relative strength of one thing to another. In turn, the strength, or value, of one thing over another can result in a rank order list where items are typically placed in a descending order from most important or most valued to least important or valued.

Another simple way that numeric information can be manipulated is to convert numbers to percentages. Again, a simple technique but powerful because people tend to understand percentages more easily than other numeric formats. For example, it is easier for people to understand a statement like "85 percent of people prefer the color orange rather than pink" as opposed to saying "188 out of 235 people prefer the color orange rather than pink." Percentages can just make information easier to understand than numbers alone so use them when needed.

Calculating averages is another number crunching method that's particularly useful when comparing, for example, ft^2 (m^2), or when calculating the average amount of time an end user spends engaging in a particular activity. Let's say you have an existing floor plan with 75 workspaces, and you want to know the average size of the workspaces. Add up the total ft^2 (m^2) of all 75 work spaces and divide by 75. This will give you the average ft^2 (m^2) of the 75 work spaces. As another example, let's say that 12 end users spend varying amounts of time doing a particular activity. If you want to determine the average amount of time end users spend on that activity, you can simply add up all of the hours, and then divide by 12.

The more number crunching methods you use, the deeper will be your understanding of the information you collected. Using the previous example of how much time 12 end users spend on a particular activity, you could determine the range of hours (the least to most amount of time spent on the activity), the total amount of time spent on the activity by all 12 employees, or the average amount of time spent on the activity (as explained earlier). In this case, your "raw data" would be as follows:

End user	Time spent on activity (hrs.)
1	4
2	2.5
3	1
4	9
5	3.5
6	2
7	3
8	3.75
9	1.5
10	2
11	2.5
12	3.5

Range – The amount of time spent on the activity by the twelve end users ranged from 1–9 hours (the lowest and highest numbers in column two).

Total – The total amount of time spent on the activity by all twelve end users is 38.25 hours (the sum of all numbers in column two).

Average – The average amount of time spent on the activity is 3.19 hours (38.25÷12=3.19).

Okay, we're done with numbers. Let's move on to assessment, the third analysis method.

Assess

Assessment is a simple, but appropriate, form of analysis for programming, and I'm confident that most of you have used some form of assessment in your lifetime. The kind of assessment that I mean involves pairs of opposite words. For example, strengths/weaknesses, pros/cons, or opportunities/constraints. I like this technique because it is a fair analysis method that "tells the whole story" about whatever it is that you're analyzing. That is, using these "opposite word" pairings, you're not just assessing the positive or good aspects about something and ignoring the negative or bad aspects; indeed, with this method you get both the good and the bad.

Although many word pairings exist, the ones most useful for analyzing programming information are strengths/weaknesses and opportunities/constraints. Strengths/weaknesses, positives/negatives, pros/cons are word pairings that mean pretty much the same thing, and can be used to assess almost any kind of information.

The opportunities/constraints word pairing is used to assess sites, buildings, and interior spaces. This is because these words (opportunities and constraints) make sense when describing features of a site or space that a designer can take advantage of, or things that may impede, or restrain the designer in some way. When using this word pairing, you can ask yourself, "Is this element, on the site or in the space, an opportunity that the designer may be able to capitalize on, or is the element a potential constraint; something that might impede the designer in some way?"

When you're assessing information using word pairings, it's a good idea to keep track of your findings by making a list beside, or attached to, whatever it is that you're assessing. As opposed to writing long, detailed explanations of your findings, the most efficient way to record your findings is to use annotation.

Annotate

Annotation, the final analysis method, is basically just "jotting down" ideas in the margins of a document, beside a drawing, at the top or bottom of a photo, or beside a chart or table. Annotation is a way of capturing important thoughts quickly; thoughts that might be lost otherwise.

In combination with assessment, annotation is a valuable way of capturing information and placing it in a location that makes sense and that is convenient. It is far easier to understand an annotated document, drawing, or chart than it is to have to look at the document, drawing, or chart; possibly decipher a legend; and then look for explanations about the document, drawing, or chart elsewhere in a document or in a binder full of documents.

The main benefit of annotation, especially during analysis when your mind may be racing with thoughts, is that annotation captures thoughts exactly when they occur. Annotations are kind of like "thought stamps" in that they are direct reflections of your thoughts that can be recorded almost instantaneously.

In the analysis phase, you'll generate many sketches, charts, tables, lists, and so on. Annotating each one is a great way to record thoughts that will be important later on in phase 3, synthesis. In the synthesis phase, you'll decide which of the many options generated through analysis will be the one or ones that make the final cut. That is, which options, whether they be zoning diagrams or charts of end user activities, are going to be included in the draft program document. Annotated diagrams or charts are going to help you make those decisions much quicker than unannotated diagrams or charts because you won't have to try and remember the strengths or weaknesses of one option over another; the strengths and weaknesses will have already been recorded using annotation and assessment analysis methods.

Draw

Freehand drawing or sketching is the fifth and final information analysis method. I'd hazard a guess that at least some of you probably haven't thought about drawing as being a form of analysis but it is. Freehand drawing is a graphic form of annotation if you will. That is, drawing is a way of recording thoughts and ideas that are in your brain just like annotation is a way of recording the same thoughts and ideas. The only difference is that drawing uses line and texture while annotation uses words and numbers. Used together, annotation and freehand drawing are a powerful duo for analyzing programmatic information.

Without a doubt, when analyzing programmatic information, you will draw something. It may be a simple bubble diagram, or a little elevation. It may even be a perspective or a floor plan. And, even though you know that programming isn't design, you should feel free to draw any kind of image that comes to mind. There is no rule to say that you can't draw a schematic floor plan in order to analyze how furniture might fit within a certain area. Just like annotation, sketching is a thought stamp that plays an important role in analyzing programmatic information.

Just in case you're wondering; analysis isn't often completed all in one sitting. That is, you may analyze for a while and then "hit a wall," unable to generate any new options or see things in different ways. At this point, turn to your attention to something else. Don't worry, all of that information will be churning away in the background of your mind, but for a few moments (or a day or two), you'll get some well-earned relief.

When you're ready to continue analysis, carry on. Analysis ends when you can't generate a single new option. At that point, though, you should have generated more than enough ideas to carry forward into synthesis, but if you haven't, then you need to go back to phase 1 and collect more information.

Analysis in Action

Now that you are aware of the things that you're focusing on in analysis (themes, options, project goals, design guidelines), and the methods that you can use to analyze information (dissect text, crunch numbers, assess, annotate, and draw), you need to know, more specifically, how to go about analysis. So, the analysis process goes something like this:

Using the holding tank form as a guide, consider the first topic in the left-hand column – site.

Re-visit all of the site-related information you collected in phase 1. Don't limit yourself to site plans only. Instead, scour your binder or digital files for anything even remotely site-related. It is always a good idea to re-visit context information (typology, precedents, trends, local context) as well.

Once you've refreshed your memory about the site, and other remotely important information, ask yourself this question, "If I'm the designer for this project, what would I want and need to know about the site?"

To answer this question, you can begin to assess the site. Using the "assess" method of opposite word pairings, identify opportunities and constraints with regard to the site. It is super important that you focus only on things that have the potential to impact the eventual interior environment.

For instance, knowing that a future building will be constructed in the area is a potential constraint for the designer because that new building may block important views or vistas that exist now, but that will not exist in the future. Thanks to you, the designer will be sure not to place the CEO's office close to the eventual new building.

Conversely, a site-related opportunity might be that an old building adjacent to the site is scheduled for demolition. Knowing this, the designer may decide to place the boardroom or some other important space in the area where the derelict building will be torn down. Once again, you, the programmer, have saved the day by providing the designer with important information that you identified through analysis.

Using the "Annotation" method, jot down your observations – both good (opportunities) and bad (constraints) – on the site plan, or on a separate piece of paper. You might even use the "Draw" analysis method to show the designer the potential impact of opportunities or constraints.

Even though I used examples about a new building going up, and a derelict one coming down, your site analysis must not be limited only to potential views from your client's space. Consider all of the information you collected in phase 1 – access to site (vehicular, bicycle, pedestrian, public); entrances to the building; major streets, rivers, or lakes; vegetation; landmarks; views and vistas to, through, and from the site; amenities and services; legal information (zoning/land usage), and so on. Also take into consideration the typology, precedents, trends, and the local context in relation to the site. What potential, if any, do these things have in relation to the site, and how could such things affect the design?

That, in a nutshell, is how analysis is done. But let me walk you through another example – a more complex one, but one that you'll appreciate. Let's say that you're about to analyze information from the perspective of the number of end users for the desired condition (the fourth topic down in the left-hand column of the holding tank form). You begin the analysis in the same way as the previous example.

Re-visit all of the end user information you collected in phase 1. Pay particular attention to the number of end users that your client predicted there would be in the desired condition. And, as is always a good practice in analysis, scour your binder or digital files for anything even remotely related to the number of end users.

Once you've refreshed your memory about end user activities and other related information, ask yourself this question, "If I'm the designer for this project, what would I want and need to know about the number of end users that are expected to occupy the space?" Unlike the previous example, to answer this question, you'll need to use almost all of the analysis techniques described earlier including dissecting text, crunching numbers, assessing, and annotating. If you do use the draw method of analysis, it will probably be drawing in the form of charts or tables.

So, beginning with the "dissect text" method of analysis, analyze all of the information that you think is relevant to the projected number of end users. Did any themes emerge that could impact the projected number of end users? For instance, is there a major economic trend emerging that could drastically affect the total number of projected end users? Have you and your client discussed this emerging financial trend? Is the trend going to result in a decreased number of end users, or an increase? If so, what would you recommend to your client in terms of sheer physical space – stay the same, rent or buy a larger space, or go with a smaller space? On and on go the questions. If it's any consolation, you only need to ask yourself questions that are pertinent to your particular project.

Next, use the "crunch numbers" method to get a handle on the actual number of projected end users. Here is where things get a little messy because this is the point at which you start considering building code information (occupancy type and occupancy load), and building area (ft^2/m^2). All three things need to be considered at the same time because each one affects the others.

To determine whether the projected number of end users is reasonable, first, identify the occupancy type. You'll do this by consulting the building code applicable to the geographic location in which your project is located. Typical occupancy types include assembly, business, educational, hazardous, institutional, mercantile, and residential (Harmon and Kennon, 2014, 64).

After determining the occupancy type (or types if you have more than one), the second step is to identify the occupancy load. This load is determined differently, depending on the building code you're using. And, if you have different occupancy types, then you will probably have different occupancy loads. Harmon and Kennon's (2014) book, *The Codes Guidebook for Interiors*, is a great resource for all things building code related. Of course, you can always consult actual building code publications if you have access to them.

At any rate, the occupancy load is the number of people who can safely occupy a space at one time. This load can be calculated in different ways, but the method used most frequently in interior design is one that's determined when you have a known square footage (m^2). This is simply because so much of the work that interior designers do is within existing spaces. To calculate the load occupancy using this method, you'll use the known area (ft^2 or m^2) of your space along with a specific load factor that is determined, in part by the occupancy type and intended function of the space or spaces. The load factor is simply the minimum amount of area needed for each occupant of a space.

For the sake of providing two examples, let's say that you have access to *Building Code X* and you want to calculate the occupancy **load** for a Y occupancy **type**. Let's also assume that you've got an available space of 4500 ft² (418.06 m²). Taking into consideration other requirements from *Building Code X*, let's say that the load factor is 18 ft² (1.67 m2), net, per occupant. To calculate the occupancy load, you simply perform this calculation:

4500 ft² (available area) ÷ 18 ft² = 250 occupants

418.06 m² (available area) ÷ 1.67 m² (load factor) = 250 occupants

In other words, your space (assuming it meets all other *Building Code X* requirements) can safely accommodate 250 end users at one time.

Let's consider another example, this time using the other method of calculating occupancy load. In this example, we'll assume that your client has not yet leased or purchased a space because she doesn't know how much space she needs. In this situation, your client wants to be able to accommodate 300 people in her new space. So, using the same Y occupancy type, and the same load factor (18 ft²/1.67 m2) as the previous example, you would do the following calculation:

300 (number of desired occupants) × 18 ft² (load factor) = 5400 ft²

300 (number of desired occupants) × 1.67 m² (load factor) = 501.68 m²

You can now tell your client that, in order to accommodate 300 end users, she requires a space that is 5400ft² (501.68 m²) net minimum, and this area does not include ancillary spaces.

Although these are rather crude examples of how to calculate occupant loads, it's plain to see why the first methods makes sense to use when you've got a known area, and why the second method makes sense to use when you've got a known number of occupants. Consult a real building code, not *Building Code X*, to determine the number of end users that your space can accommodate, or the amount of area required to accommodate the desired number of occupants. Real building codes also explain net and gross area.

Once you've crunched the numbers, you may need to ask yourself some questions about end user numbers. Have you or your client assumed that more end users will be able to be accommodated in the space than the building code allows? If you reduce the number of end users to meet building code requirements, what will be the impact on the end design and on your client's business or organization?

Still on the "more complex" example dealing with number of end users, let's move on to the "assessment" and "annotation" methods of analysis. Pairs of opposite words can be used to assess some of the options you've generated with regard to the projected number of end users. For example, let's say that you've generated several scenarios for your client to consider with regard to the number of end users.

Scenario One: Current projection – 300 end users with a 10,000 ft^2 (929.03m^2)
Scenario Two: Five-year projection – 250 end users with a 10,000 ft^2 (929.03m^2)
Scenario Three: Ten-year projection – 150 end users with a 10,000 ft^2 (929.03m^2)

You can assess each scenario using the pros/cons word pairing because it makes the most sense. Ask yourself, "What are the pros of having only 250 end users five years from now? And, what are the cons? Use the annotate method to record your thoughts. A pro might be that your client will require less space in five years but the related con is that your client will have to move to a new location, or continue paying to lease space that is not being used. Another pro might be that the company workflow has become more efficient. The con might be that employees are feeling stressed from high workloads and are missing more days of work which, in the end, is costing your client more money, and so on.

And finally, the last analysis method – drawing. Tables, pie charts, histograms, or similar images can be helpful, not just for understanding the options yourself, but for explaining the options to your client as well.

As you can see by the two examples explained above, analysis is no easy task. It's deep, dark, and messy – but only if you let it get that way. If you take each topic on the holding tank form one-by-one, and try to complete a thorough analysis of that topic before moving on to the next one, your entire analysis phase should proceed smoothly. This is not to say that you can only analyze each topic once, but you may find that while you're analyzing one topic, ideas arise about other topics. Simply jot those ideas down quickly, keep focused on the topic you're analyzing, and then move on to the other topics. You'll have the quick notes that you jotted down to remind you what you were thinking.

The most important thing in analysis is to remember to consider information from the designer's point of view, because ultimately, it is the designer who is going to use the program you create. Don't analyze information that doesn't need to be analyzed. Don't include information that won't help the designer. And, finally, keep track of major findings or important ideas on the holding tank form.

Analysis Products

At the end of the analysis phase, you'll have two types of information – a pile of messy drawings, sketches, lists, calculations, charts, and annotated drawing – and a holding tank form. Messy drawings are a product of analysis because, when the ideas, possibilities, and options start to flow, there is a tendency to move very quickly in order to capture everything (Figures 5.1–5.3). It is quite possible that many of the drawings that you generate will be downright illegible to anyone else but you. The messiness doesn't matter though, because the analysis phase is about idea generation, not about communicating beautiful diagrams for publication.

In order to facilitate quick thinking, I highly recommend doing analysis by hand rather than on the computer. One more thing – do not re-create the messy drawings using a computer program. Doing so is a waste of time because, at this point, you'll have way too many options and you won't be sure, just yet, which ones you might use for the draft program. Having said all of this, the only analysis product that you may want to reproduce is the holding tank form.

The holding tank form – that you should have been using throughout the entire analysis process – is an essential analysis product. Now that you're at the end of the analysis phase, it's time to take a good look at that form. Does it include all of the important themes, options, project objectives, and design guidelines that emerged throughout the process? If not, then take a few moments to record any missing thoughts, and if necessary, reproduce the form so that it is legible. The legible holding tank form will be your starting point for phase 3.

Table 5.3 provides a summary that shows the kinds of products that can result from analysis of each topic on the holding tank form. Knowing the types

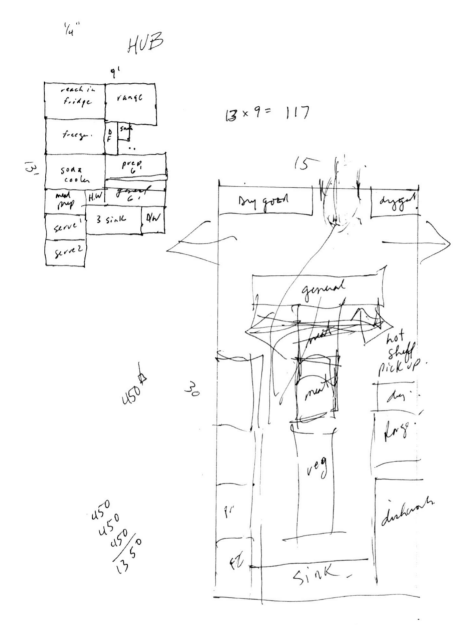

Figure 5.1 Messy analysis product 1: Block diagram, schematic plan, calculations (by author).

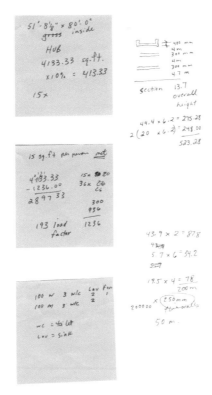

Figure 5.2 Messy analysis product 2: Calculations (by author).

of products that can result from each topic provides not-subtle clues as to which methods are appropriate for analyzing each topic.

Summary

This chapter explained the complex process of analysis but, in doing so, attempted to keep the process as simple as possible. Just five methods of analysis were described including: dissecting text, crunching numbers, assessment, annotation, and drawing. Highly detailed examples were provided in the latter part of the chapter explaining how each method could be used. A holding tank form was introduced early in the chapter as an analysis tool and product that could be used to help you keep track of important ideas throughout the analysis process. In addition to the holding tank form, the chapter emphasized the fact that analysis does result

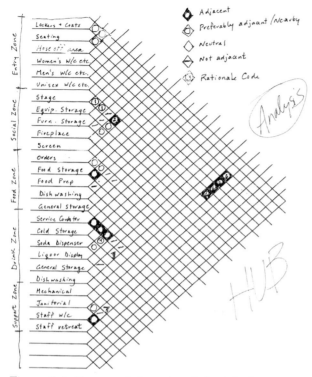

Figure 5.3 Messy analysis product 3: Spatial adjacency matrix (by author).

Table 5.3 Information analysis topics and products (by author)

Analysis topics	Analysis products
Themes	Word clouds
	Ranked lists
	Frequency counts
	Percentages
	Tables
	Lists
Site	Bullet point description of the site's main features
	Site plan or plans with opportunities/constraints identified
	Photos (annotated)

Table 5.3 (Cont.)

Analysis topics	Analysis products
	Site elevations or sections
	Maps of the site and larger context (at different scales)
Building and space	Bullet point description building and space
	Floor Plans of existing space with opportunities/constraints identified
	Demolition plans with annotation
	Base plan
	Sun path diagrams to analyze the impact of natural light within the interior at different times of day, year, etc.. Could impact zoning, and eventual furniture placement, window treatments, lighting, and HVAC
	Elevations or sections
	Photos (annotated)
Workflow	Organizational chart options (assessed and annotated). Used to communicate the relationship between job positions and/or to demonstrate hierarchy within a company or organization
	Affinity diagrams (assessed and annotated)
	Workflow charts with pros/cons identified
	Ranked or prioritized list of workflow charts with rationale
Number of end users	Messy sheets of calculations
	Tables
	Charts (pie, bar, histogram, etc.)
End user activities	Sociograms (used to indicate where and how often people communicate with one another) (annotated, and positives/negatives identified)
	Affinity diagrams (assessed and annotated)
	Tables showing activity analysis
	Messy numeric calculations
	Word clouds showing frequency of activities

(*continued*)

Table 5.3 (cont.)

Analysis topics	Analysis products
Activity zone requirements	Charts with FFE, lighting, plumbing, electrical needs identified
	Block diagrams showing FFE to scale
Area requirements	Messy calculations showing occupancy type, occupancy load, area
	Block diagrams of area options
	Tables with area totals, circulation, gross, net totals
Spatial adjacencies	Spatial relationship options with rationale/assessment strength/weakness
Zoning	Zoning options for each floor (annotated and assessed strengths/weaknesses)
	Stacking option diagrams (vertical zoning) (annotated and assessed)
	Axonometric, isometric, plan oblique, section sketches analyzing vertical spatial relationships (annotated)
	Acoustic/visual privacy zones identified
	Private, semi-private, semi-public, public zones identified
Circulation	Main entrance, emergency exits
	Major, minor, infrequent circulation paths or public/private, or public/employee circulation
	Vertical circulation
	Floor plans with egress paths

in many messy drawings, calculations, sketches, and other information. This messy information, however, contains options and ideas that, along with the holding tank form, are critical for the next programming phase, synthesis.

References

Harmon, Sharon K. and Katherine E. Kennon. 2014. *The Codes Guidebook for Interiors*. 6th ed. Hoboken, NJ: Wiley.

Kumlin, Robert R. 1995. *Architectural Programming: Creative Techniques for Design Professionals*. New York: McGraw-Hill.

Chapter 6

SYNTHESIS

Synthesis is not simply a matter of taking products from previous programming phases, plunking them into a document, and calling it a day (or a draft, in this case). Rather, synthesis is a thoughtful process in which you combine two or more things to create something new. In this case, that something new is the draft program document; the one that describes your client's desired condition, and the one that you will evaluate, revise, and then format before presenting it to your instructor or client. This chapter describes one simple method for helping you establish priorities and choose content that will result in your draft program document.

Methods

The one method discussed here – constant comparison – may seem insufficient for such an important thing as synthesis. And, maybe it is, but at least it's consistent with the minimal number of other methods in the Student Programming Model (SPM). As you're aware, my objective in writing this book was to provide a practical process for programming; a process that students like you could actually use. And so, the limited number of programming methods is intentional.

The main product of the analysis phase – the holding tank form – is the thing that you'll use as a starting point for the synthesis phase. Using the constant comparison method to assess the holding tank, and other information, you'll establish priorities. In turn, those priorities will help you make decisions about which content to include in your draft program document.

Constant Comparison

Synthesis begins with a rather grueling method called constant comparison. It's the same technique that was explained, briefly, in the dissecting text (content analysis) method. Necessary at this point, though, is more thorough explanation of constant comparison.

Constant comparison is a method that some researchers use to analyze qualitative data. Ever since I first read about the method, I have maintained that it is exactly what interior designers do, over and over again, when they are in the throes of design. Of course, designers don't call what they do "constant comparison;" they just call it design. But, as they're designing, designers are constantly asking themselves, "If I do this, what will happen to that?" And, "If I do that, what will happen to this?" These questions are exactly the questions that need to be asked when using the constant comparison method; consider the consequences of an action before taking that action.

The constant comparison technique is simply enough in terms of its mechanics (the way it operates). What makes the method difficult, however, is the number of variables that need to be taken into consideration before a decision can be made. In content analysis, the variables were all of the code categories that you created. In synthesis, the variables are all of the ideas from the holding tank as well as the project goals and assumptions that you and your client (or just you) established in phase 1.

At first, comparing all of these things is mind-boggling but, in programming and design, once you make the first decision, each decision that follows is easier to make. That's because, after the first decision is made the program or design takes a certain direction; all that the other decisions need to do is support that direction. Clearly then, there is much to be considered before making that super important first decision because that decision will shape the remainder of the program and have a tremendous effect on the eventual designed environment. No pressure here at all (sarcasm intended)!

Provided next is a brief explanation of how the constant comparison method can be used to prioritize the many ideas and issues that have emerged up to this point in the programming process.

Priorities

You're probably wondering, "What exactly is it that needs to be prioritized? Isn't the holding tank my list of priorities?" Well, no, the holding tank isn't a list of priorities; rather, it's a list of really important ideas that resulted from analysis. And now, it's all of the ideas on that list that need to be prioritized. So, using the constant comparison method, you'll identify priorities by simply taking one holding tank idea at a time, considering the consequences of making that idea or issue a priority (by comparing that single idea to the all of the other ideas on the form and to the project goals and assumptions) and then deciding whether or not that idea should be a priority.

The process of going through each idea, one-by-one, is taxing but it's what you need to do in order to proceed with the rest of the programming process. So, there's no magic here, no special instructions or advice; instead, just think about the importance of each holding tank idea compared to other holding tank ideas, and to other important things like the project goals.

Don't worry if this exercise takes a fair amount of time; if done thoroughly, it should. Once you've completed the process of generating priorities, you're probably thinking that you're done with the constant comparison method. Unfortunately, you're not. You should do one more comparison to ensure that the items on your list are in an order that you're happy with. Although grueling, the benefit of doing one more round of comparison is that you'll be über confident about your list of priorities, and super-excited because your draft program now has a justified and specific direction.

With a specific direction, or purpose in mind, you can now consider some of the options for content; that is, content that could be included in your draft program. After reading about the options, a few words of advice are provided in terms of the content order for your draft program.

Content Options

This section of the chapter provides brief descriptions of some of the content that you may decide to include in your draft program, along with format suggestions (e.g., prose, list, chart, floor plan, section). The content and format suggestions are not definitive or exclusive; that is, there are many more content options and formats for communicating programmatic content.

Abstract

Suggested format: Prose

If an abstract is required, develop three short paragraphs describing the project purpose, the programming process, and the programming product/s.

Executive Summary

Suggested format: Prose, lists, charts

Longer than an abstract, an executive summary is, essentially a mini program document meant to explain all of the critical parts of the longer document that it represents. It is not normally included in student programs. See the *Extreme Toy Hauler Mobile Showroom* (Appendix C) for an example.

Table of Contents, List of Figures, List of Tables

Suggested Format: Lists

Self-explanatory. Be sure to give credit for images that are not your own either on the list of figures or images, or on a separate "credits" list.

Project Overview

Suggested format: Prose, photos

Include: the name of your client's business; the street address or location of the project; the town, city, region, province, state or country in which the project is located; project purpose; the main programmatic activities that will occur in the space; the total number of primary end users expected to use the space; a brief building description (i.e., number of stories); and total ft² (m²). A photo or two is optional. Other information can be added as appropriate.

Anybody at all, not just stakeholders, should be able to read this description and understand what or who the project is for, what occupants are going to do in the space, where the project is located, and how big or small the space is.

Project Goals, Assumptions, and Objectives
Suggested format: Prose, bulleted or prioritized lists, tables

Use information from phases 1–2 to craft concise statements that describe the project goals, assumptions, and project objectives. Remember, goals are usually not measurable but project objectives are. The *Blackthorn Live/Create* program (Appendix A) provides examples of goals, assumptions, and objectives.

Site, Building, and Space Descriptions
Suggested format: Prose, maps, architectural drawings, lists, charts, tables, photos

Provide the designer with enough information about the site, building, and space so that he understands the context in which the project will exist. Use information from phases 1–2, keeping in mind that you may want to re-produce some of the drawings or photos that you collected in phase 1.

Provide brief introductory descriptions for the site, the building, and the space. For the site, include: maps, site plans, or roof plans; site sections; a benefits and constraints assessment; and photos. Similarly, for the building and space, provide: floor plans; sections; a list of building features including construction type, building systems including vertical circulation systems; sections, a benefits and constraints assessment; and photos.

Building Code Information
Suggested format: Prose, lists, tables, schematic diagrams

At minimum, include the occupancy type (classification) and occupancy load. You may also wish to include any special accessibility, life safety, or other guidelines and codes information depending on the nature of your project.

Client Description
Suggested format: Prose, lists, tables, charts

Provide a concise written description of your client's business, industry, or organization. Include your client's mission statement, core values, future plans, and organizational structure diagram. History can be included if it's relevant. Use information collected in phase 1 to generate this description.

Workflow

Suggested format: Infographics, sociograms, affinity diagrams, tables, lists, charts

Briefly describe how people, information, and products move through your client's facility. Briefly describe who communicates with who, where, when, and how frequently. You may wish to include both existing and desired work flow diagrams.

End User Profiles, Needs, and Activities

Suggested format: Prose, lists, tables, charts

End user descriptions, needs, and activities are usually communicated in a single table although you'll likely have separate tables for primary, secondary, and tertiary end users. The *Blackthorn Live/Create* program provides an example of a detailed end user profile. *The HUB* (Appendix B) provides an example of end user profiles for a multi-purpose space where there are a variety of end users.

Activity Zone Requirements

Suggested format: Prose, lists, tables

Typically, these requirements focus on furniture, fixtures, and equipment (FFE), but other requirements can be included as well (e.g., lighting, plumbing, special requirements). Most often, this information is presented in a table format.

Area Requirements

Suggested format: Prose, lists, block diagrams, charts

Usually presented as a one-page summary of all area (ft^2/m^2) estimates. The chart or list can consist of numbers only, or can include numbers and block diagrams (proportional squares). Must always include the total area for circulation (as a percentage and as a number), as well as the grand total. *The HUB* (Appendix B) includes a summary of area requirements in the form of block diagrams.

Spatial Adjacency Matrices

Suggested format: Matrices, lists, tables, legends

The matrix is more meaningful to the designer if rational or "reason" codes are included. See Edward White's (1986) *Space Adjacency Analysis: Diagraming Information for Architectural Design* book for an excellent explanation about spatial analysis methods including adjacency matrixes, bubble diagrams, and zoning diagrams. Always include a legend with no more than four levels of adjacency indicated. Spatial relationship matrixes can also be created to show vertical relationships. Including an assessment of strengths/weaknesses is a good way to summarize the matrix.

Zoning and Stacking Diagrams

Suggested format: bubble diagram, schematic diagrams, legends, lists, annotation, floor plans, sections

Zoning or bubble diagrams are used to show the spatial relationships and adjacencies determined with the spatial adjacency matrixes. Most zoning diagrams are done within the confines of the known space (i.e., on a floor plan), but, if your client's building is not yet built, zoning diagrams are still possible to create. I call the first kind of zoning diagrams, "practical" because they are done within a defined, known area, and I call the second kind of zoning diagrams "theoretical" because they are done without any building restrictions.

Vertical zoning diagrams are often called stacking diagrams and are created to understand and explain vertical spatial relationships.

Circulation Diagrams

Suggested format: bubble diagrams, schematics, stacking diagrams, floor plans, sections, legends, lists

Circulation diagrams are usually straight forward but can be complicated when you have end users whose paths must not cross at any time. For example, in a court house, you would not want criminals crossing paths with judges.

Typically, major and minor circulation are indicated, but additional levels or types of circulation can be included as well. Again, circulation diagrams can be done both horizontally and vertically.

If the zoning and circulation diagrams are relatively straightforward, and not cluttered visually, both diagrams can be combined on one.

Design Guidelines

Suggested Format: prose, issue, objective, concept

The phrase "design guidelines" is one that I use to describe unique issues that emerge throughout the each and every programming process. In effect, these guidelines act as a summary of the program because that they identify the most important **design** issues that the designer needs to address as he moves into conceptual and schematic design.

In the previous chapter, I explained a little bit about how I borrowed the issues, objectives, and concepts idea from Robert Kumlin (1995). I'll finish that explanation here. The main difference between how Kumlin (1995) uses his framework, and how I use it, centers on the word "issues." Kumlin (1995) considers issues to be those recurring, somewhat generic, topics that arise, time after time, in many or most architectural projects. I consider issues to be quite the opposite because I think of them as unique topics; things that make your project different from every other project. Other than issues, I agree with Kumlin's description of objectives and concepts, and highly recommend that you formulate your own by following Kumlin's (1995) method.

An example of a design guideline for *The HUB* (Appendix B) is as follows:

Issue: Durability
Objective: *The Hub* and its furnishings should be able to withstand mud, snow, and water
Concept: Consider installing waterproof materials where ever possible

Schematic Concept Drawings
Suggested Format: hand drawn or digital floor plans sections, perspectives, axonometrics, sketches

Schematic concept drawings, if included in your program, often follow, or accompany design guidelines, although they can be placed anywhere in the document. The purpose of the images is to simply express your ideas about the space that is, by now, beginning to take shape. Designers are not obligated to use the drawings but the drawings can give designers a good idea of the direction that the programmer thinks the project ought to lean toward.

References
Suggested format: Prose
Self-explanatory.

Appendices

Suggested format: Prose, lists, charts, tables, drawings, etc.

Anything that is important but not critical can be included here.

Content Format and Order

Now that you've considered all of the possible content that could be included in your draft program, you need to make decisions about which content you will actually include, and the format and order in which the content will be arranged. The two most common programming formats are: activity zone information (room data) sheets, and topic-by-topic. The difference between the two is that, with the activity zone sheets, all of the content pertaining to each activity area is contained on one piece of paper, whereas with the topic-by-topic format, all of the content pertaining to each major topic in the program is included together in one section.

Content in the *Blackthorn Live/Create*, and *The HUB* programs (Appendix A–B) is arranged in a topic-by-topic format. *The Extreme Toy Hauler Mobile Showroom* program (Appendix C) uses what I call a hybrid format because it includes some topic-by-topic content and some data sheet content.

There are no restrictions in terms of the content to be included in your program, the format to be used, or the order in which content must be arranged. To help you make decisions about these three things, you need to return to the priorities you established earlier. Do any of the priorities suggest that certain content should be included or that content should be arranged in a specific order or format? While your list of priorities probably isn't going to jump right out and provide you with an answer, you can usually make at least some loose connection between priorities, content, format, and content order.

Besides the project priorities, another thing that may help you decide on the content, format, and order is the designer; the person who is going to use your program to begin conceptual or schematic design. How is the designer most likely to use the final program document? Would it be beneficial to arrange content topic-by-topic, on activity zone data sheets, or in a hybrid fashion? In your case, you'll probably be the designer who ends up using your program so you can make choices based on your personal preferences. If you aren't the designer though, what would be the best way to arrange content so that the designer can understand the project and find what she needs quickly?

Once you've decided on a format (topic-by-topic, activity zone information sheets, or hybrid), you need to consider the specific pieces of information described earlier in the chapter. In what order, exactly, will each piece of information be arranged? I strongly recommend, of course, a feed-forward or logical order. That is to say, content that is arranged in a way that allows stakeholders (clients, designers, perhaps end users) to understand how the project came to be, what the purpose of the project is, who the project is for, where the project will be located, and so on.

While considering which pieces of information to include in your draft, remember that program documents should always be as brief as possible, but should not exclude material for the sake of brevity. As you're considering content to include, ask yourself this one simple question, "Does the designer need to know this?" If the answer is yes, then include the information in the draft; if the answer is no, then do not include the information.

Synthesis Products

The draft document focuses exclusively on your real or hypothetical client's desired condition. Although the product of this phase is only a draft program, you'll want to approach it as though you're creating the final document. That way, you aren't likely to say things to yourself like, "I'll add that missing piece of information later on when I'm assembling the final document." All this does is cause you to go through the evaluation phase again. Also, because the product of synthesis is a draft document, and you can see the end in sight, you may be tempted to start digitizing hand drawn information or formatting charts and tables. While this is a good idea, don't spend countless hours perfecting each table, chart, or drawing for the draft. Wait until you've completed the final draft, evaluated the draft, and made any revisions necessary. The final digital drawings can be perfected in the final programming phase – communication.

Summary

This chapter began by explaining how the products of analysis – in conjunction with a labor-intensive method called constant comparison – can be used to determine programming priorities. These priorities, it was explained, are needed in order to make decisions about the content, format, and content order that will give shape to the draft program document. Next, the chapter provided brief descriptions of some of the content that could be included in a draft program. And, finally, suggestions were provided in the last part of the chapter with regard to selecting the format, content, and content order for the draft program.

References

Kumlin, Robert R. 1995. *Architectural Programming: Creative Techniques for Design Professionals*. New York: McGraw-Hill.

White, Edward T. 1986. *Space Adjacency Analysis: Diagramming Information for Architectural Design*. Tucson, AZ: Architectural Media Ltd.

Chapter 7

EVALUATION AND REVISION, COMMUNICATION

This chapter includes explanations of two programming phases – evaluation and revision, and communication. In keeping with the practical nature of the Student Programming Model (SPM), the evaluation and revision methods are straightforward and relatively simple. The same can be said for the part of the chapter that describes communication. Evaluation, revision, and communication are the three last things you need to consider as you prepare your final program document.

Evaluation

The fourth phase of the SPM involves evaluating, and potentially revising the outcome of the previous phase; the draft document. As is the case in previous phases of programming, it is important to pause and reflect on your current position. In this case, however, pausing to reflect on the synthesized draft document is critical. It is your last chance to make changes before presenting the final program document to your instructor, client, or other stakeholders.

Review

The first thing that needs to be evaluated is the content of the synthesized draft document from phase 3. Obviously, a review of the draft is all that is required here;

however, the review will be more thorough if you've taken at least one day off in between completing the draft and reviewing it.

Is everything included that needs to be, or are some important pieces of information missing? Is there any information that could make the document stronger, or easier to understand? If the answer to either of these questions is yes, then now is the time to add the missing or additional information.

By this point in the programming process, you may find it difficult to be objective because you've been thinking about, and looking at the program for so long. It may be helpful, then, to have someone who is not familiar with your project read your draft. Preferably, this person will be a student or practitioner because they will understand what information a program should contain, or will know what information a designer needs in order to begin concept and schematic design. If you don't have access to anyone with a design background, get someone else to review it, because any objective set of eyes will be helpful at this point.

Compare

Once you are satisfied that all of the content is included, the next thing to evaluate is the degree of congruency between the project goals, the project objectives, and the design guidelines. Each of these things should describe your program in a slightly different way, but they should all agree with one another. Furthermore, all three things should reflect the list of priorities that you so painstakingly generated in phase 3. Although not critical, you could also evaluate the degree of consistency between the design guidelines and the schematics (if you've included any in your draft).

If the goals, objectives, and guidelines are consistent, then no revisions are necessary. If there are discrepancies between any of them, then you need to consider whether or not they should be brought into alignment, and if so, how. This may require discussion with your instructor, client, classmates, or others.

Revision

In Chapter 5, I said that I would explain why modifying project objectives this late in the game is acceptable. Here is my explanation. Modifying project objectives after the draft program is complete is not a bad thing – especially for students. Modifying objectives demonstrates that you've uncovered or determined new information that is important enough to cause the original project objectives to be modified, and having the opportunity to modify things is exactly the benefit of evaluation. You, your instructor, your client (if you have one), and your peers can help you identify how your project's priorities have evolved throughout the programming process.

Make any and all revisions necessary before moving on to the final step of the SPM – communicating the final program document.

Communication

This is it. You've made it this far. So, what is this one last thing that you need to consider? Well, it's called communication, and it requires you to make just a few more decisions about your audience and the final document format. What I mean by format is the graphic layout – the page orientation, font style and size, print color, etc. And, while it is completely acceptable to forego any kind of "special" formatting, even the most basic formatting can make a difference in how the document is perceived and how the contents are understood.

Unlike all of the phases prior to this one, the communicate phase doesn't really have any methods associated with it other than the rather obvious methods of choosing; that is, choosing the format for your final program document.

Audience

Knowing your audience is crucial when trying to determine an appropriate format for any document, not just programming documents. In your case, the only audience you might have is your instructor. Perhaps your peers, friends, or family will be interested audiences, but if you're assembling the program as an assignment, then naturally, your instructor is going to be your main audience.

Your instructor's expectations trump any advice that follows; however, in the event that your instructor has provided little in the way of assignment requirements, or if you happen to be working on a thesis or practicum project where your program isn't being graded per se, then the information that follows may be helpful.

In the event that you have a real client, you should consider what format might be best for that client. For instance, would your client expect a straight forward, "no frills" document, or would she appreciate something a little more creative?

Does your client have visual impairments that would necessitate making careful choices with regard to font size or color? These kinds of things need to be taken seriously, because if your client can't read the document, then it's of little use to her. Granted, many documents today are shared electronically, which of course, would enable someone with visual impairments to view the program without difficulty.

And last but not least is you. Are you the main audience for your final program? Will you actually have to use the program in studio, or is the document just to be handed in and then never read again? If you'll need to use the document, then what are your own preferences for the graphic format? Do you prefer a portrait or landscape orientation? Do you like a lot of color on your document or do you find a lot of color to be distracting?

Purpose

In addition to the intended audience, how you communicate your final program depends on the circumstances for which you created it. For example, if your program is a rather minor one that needs to be completed for studio in which the focus is on design not programming, then you may not want, nor need to spend much time formatting a final document at all; perhaps the revised draft will suffice. If your program is a course assignment, then your instructor may expect to receive a highly polished final document, in which case you'll want to spend some time on formatting. If your program is part of a practicum, it may exist as a chapter within a book rather than as a stand-alone document. In this case the format may depend on how the practicum book, as a whole, is formatted.

The contents of a program vary depending on the purpose of the program. For example, in situations where your program appears as a chapter in a book, some students remove the site, building, and space descriptions from the program and place that information in a different part of the book. This is completely acceptable. Again, which content you include in a program is entirely up to you.

Time

Besides audience and program purpose, the one last major consideration that will affect the format you choose is time. Whether or not you have time to do any special formatting to your final program is something only you will know. But, if you have great graphic design skills and can format documents fairly quickly, then you may decide to make the effort. If you're not confident about your graphic design or digital formatting skills, then it's probably best to just word process the final document.

Summary

This chapter described the last two phases of the SPM – evaluation and revision, and communication. As explained in the chapter, evaluation requires you to simply review and compare your draft program document from phase 3. Particularly important to evaluate is the degree of congruency between project goals, project objectives, and design guidelines. If no inconsistencies are found between the goals, objectives, and guidelines, then no revisions are required. If inconsistencies are discovered, then revisions must be made before producing the final program document.

The final program document can be communicated in a variety of ways. Before selecting a final format, however, you need to consider the intended audience, the purpose for which the program was created, and the amount of time you have available. Whether the final document is a simple black and white one created with a word processing program, or a full color beautifully designed document created with graphic design software – the choice is yours to make.

Chapter 8

SUMMARY AND CONCLUSION

Beyond the basic structure of the SPM, the model is unique because it: (a) stresses people and activities as the basis for making programmatic decisions, and communicating programmatic information; (b) promotes programming as a catalyst for change (Silverstein and Jacobson, 1978); (c) includes a unique information analysis form called the Holding Tank; and (d) includes design guidelines, something not included in other programming models. With the SPM's unique features and simple framework, I believe that I achieved what I set out to do which was to create a practical model that would enable students to produce high-quality programs in a reasonable amount of time.

Summary

The programming model described in this book represents an amalgamation of ideas from authors who wrote about programming before I did, and from my own thoughts and experiences related to teaching programming to undergraduate students. The main objective in creating the model, and in writing this book, was to offer students an alternative method for programming interior environments. I wanted the SPM to be different than other interior design programming models though; otherwise, what would be the point? All of the existing books about programming interior environments are excellent, and there was no way that I could improve upon their high standards, so I opted to develop what I think is a reasonable alternative model for programming interior environments, and that is the Student Programming Model (SPM).

To provide some context for the SPM, I started the book off with an overview of the interior design process showing how programming fits into that process. That was followed by an interesting story of how modern-day programming came to be. In the third chapter, I provided an analysis of seven interior design programming models that were available in published literature. Lastly, I introduced the SPM and explained how it fit with the other seven models.

The SPM consists of four components: methods, phases, topics, and products. The five phases – collection, analysis, synthesis, evaluation and revision, and communication – are the backbone of the model; they dictate the topics and methods needed to generate the desired product for each phase. With practicality and students' limited time in mind, the methods associated with each phase were designed to be quite basic and easy to use. In fact, none of them require anything beyond simple logic and basic math. Products resulting from each phase are clear and simple: organized information, a holding tank form, a draft program, a revised draft program, and a final program.

Beyond the basic structure of the SPM, some of the features that make the model unique are that it:

- Stresses people and activities as the basis for making programmatic decisions, and communicating programmatic information
- Promotes programming as a catalyst for change (Silverstein and Jacobson, 1978)
- Includes a unique information analysis form called the Holding Tank
- Includes design guidelines, something not included in other programming models

With the SPM's unique features and simple framework, I believe that I achieved what I set out to do, which again, was to create a practical model that would enable students to produce high-quality programs in a reasonable amount of time.

Conclusion

Ever since the 1950s, when publications about modern-era programming first surfaced, many authors predicted that technology would have a tremendous impact on programming. Despite the enormous technological advancements made since the 1950s, I don't think anyone today would say that technology has had a revolutionary effect on programming.

Yes, advancements have certainly been made, and there exist today numerous software programs and apps that can make some parts of the programming process a lot easier to accomplish than they were in the past. But in my opinion, no matter how "good" technology gets, programming still, and always will, require programmers who can empathize with the people who eventually occupy the interiors that they program. So for now, I will continue to teach using my practical SPM, and remain hopeful that technology never completely overtakes programming.

Reference

Silverstein, Murray and Max Jacobson. 1978. Restructuring the hidden program: Toward an architecture of social change. In *Facility Programming: Methods and Applications*, ed. Wolfgang F. E. Preiser, 7–26. Stroudsburg, PA: Dowden, Hutchinson & Ross.

APPENDIX A

Figure A01 *Blackthorn Live/Create Program*, Bristol, UK (unless noted, all Appendix A figures by Tiffany Maybituin; all Appendix A tables by author)

TABLE OF CONTENTS

BLACKTHORN LIVE/CREATE PROGRAM

Project Overview

Kate Blackthorn is a 37-year-old graphic designer who has three primary passions in life – graphic design, cats, and scooters. Recently, Kate purchased a commercial building in Bristol, UK. The building is located in a vibrant part of the city known as Stokes Croft. Kate plans to renovate the three-story building into a live/create environment.

Project Goals

- To design a long-term live/create environment that is flexible and that can be reconfigured as Kate's preferences or needs change
- To design an environment that reflects Kate's values including freedom, creativity, spontaneity, honesty, and order

Project Objectives

- To create an environment of contrasts that reflects Kate's character
- To create a flexible environment that can be altered with little effort
- To create a secure environment for Kate's pricey investments including her graphic design and airbrush equipment as well as her vintage scooter collection

Project Assumptions

- The building systems (mechanical and plumbing) will be replaced
- The renovations will satisfy all building code requirements including those for accessibility
- The client may eventually have a partner but will not have children
- The third floor will be for living activities, the middle floor for graphic design work, and the lower floor for airbrush work, scooter storage, and entertaining
- If there is not enough space, Kate's vintage scooter collection will be stored off site

Site Description

Kate Blackthorn's building is located in a conservation area of Bristol, UK known as Stokes Croft (Figures A02–A03). According to Smith (2018), Stokes Croft is "a cultural hub, it's a blight on the city, it's a state of mind" (para. 1). Kate is inspired by this

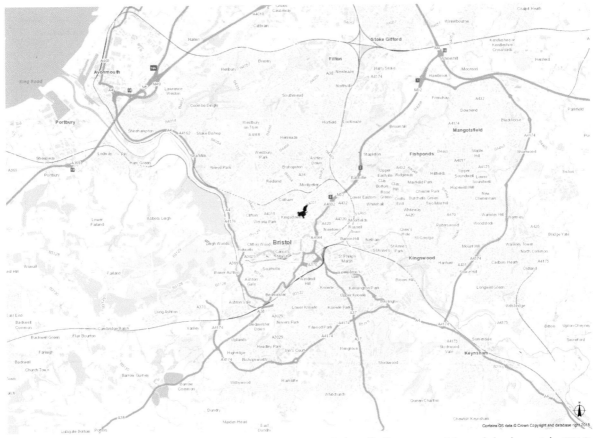

Figure A02 Bristol, UK (contains OS data © Crown copyright and database right 2018. Used with permission from City Design, Bristol City Council)

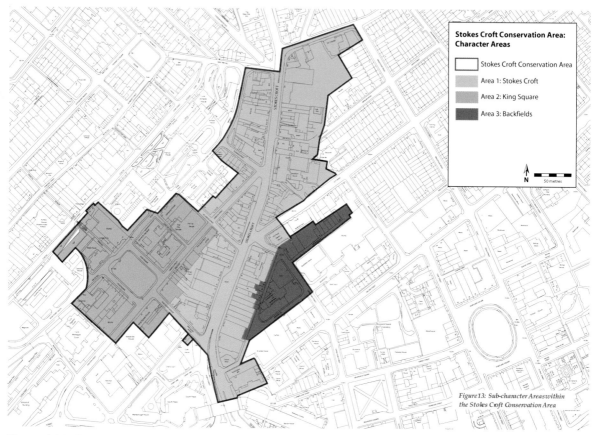

Figure A03 Conservation Area 19: Stokes Croft, Bristol, UK (contains OS data © Crown copyright and database right 2018. Used with permission from City Design, Bristol City Council)

quirky location. She draws energy from the dynamic, creative area that "is best known for its street art, including early examples of Banksy's work" (Smith, inset after para. 6).

Source: Smith, Joseph. 2018. What is Stokes Croft? www.bristolpost.co.uk/ news/bristol-news/what-is-stokes-croft-1155993

Site Opportunities

The location is easily accessed by pedestrians, bicycles, and motor vehicles. Friends, family, and clients can get to Kate's place quite easily.

Off the lane, there is a small parking area. To increase the parking area for friends, family, and clients, a portion of the extremely long first floor could be demolished.

Site Constraints

Because the building is "sandwiched" between two other buildings, the second and third floors only have windows facing the street and the lane.

Building Description

The three-story building, located at 44 XYZ Street, is constructed of brick and timber, and is designated as mixed-use. A notable feature of the building is the long ground (first) floor; it measures 44.4m long by 6.2m wide (outside). In contrast, the two upper floors are 20m long by 6.2m wide (outside). The height (not including parapet walls) is 13.6m from the ground to the top side of the roof.

The ground level is 250.23m2, while the second and third levels are 111.15m^2 (inside). The **total interior area** of all three floors is **472.53m^2**. The first floor is 5m high (from the floor to the top of the second story floor). The second and third floors are 4.3m high (from the floor to the top of the floor to the top of the floor or roof above).

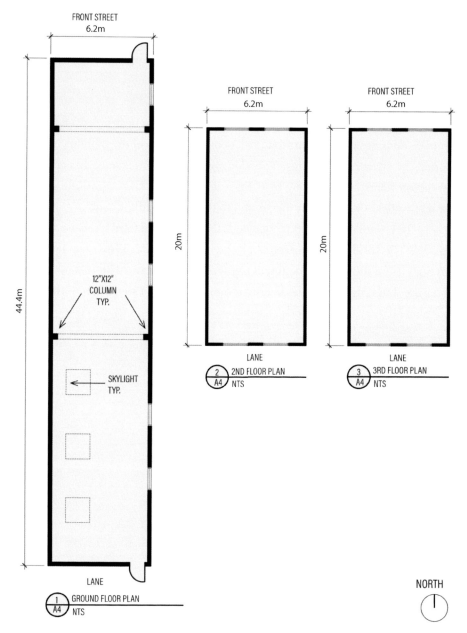

Figure A04 Floor plans

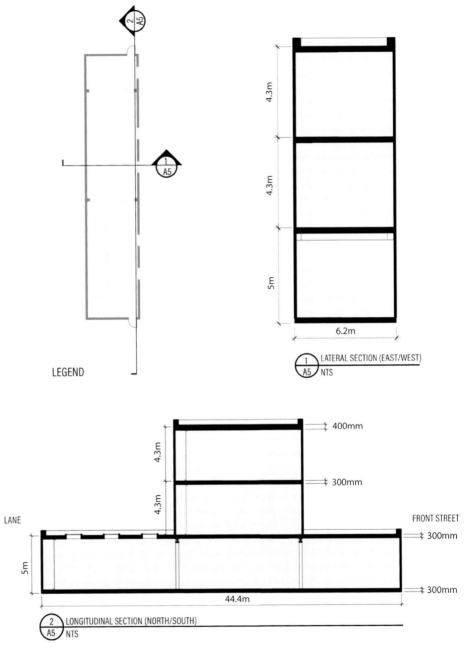

LEGEND

4.3m

4.3m

5m

6.2m

1 LATERAL SECTION (EAST/WEST)
A5 NTS

4.3m

400mm

4.3m

300mm

LANE

FRONT STREET

300mm

5m

300mm

44.4m

2 LONGITUDINAL SECTION (NORTH/SOUTH)
A5 NTS

Figure A05 Sections

Building Opportunities

- Three levels will allow for visual and acoustical separation of activities; an objective identified early on in the project
- The large interior area (470m²+) should accommodate Kate's many activities including her vintage scooter collection
- The building is structurally sound since the previous owner added 300mm x 300mm steel beams and columns on the ground floor to support the upper two levels
- The 20m+ long roof, at the rear of the ground floor level, could be utilized for a substantial deck area off of the second level
- In addition to large windows on the street facing elevation, the ground level has five windows on the northwest elevation and three skylights on the northeast ceiling
- The building has been gutted already since the previous owner was going to renovate but, unfortunately, went bankrupt

Building Constraints

- As noted earlier, on the second and third floors, there is limited access to natural light. Perhaps a skylight might be considered for the third floor
- All new mechanical systems will be required
- An elevator will need to be installed to meet Kate's potential future need for vertical access using a mobility scooter or wheelchair
- New staircases will need to be installed throughout

End User Profiles, Needs, and Activities

Kate Blackthorn is a woman of opposites. She does airbrush work, hand drawing, painting, and digital graphic art. She does very small and very large hand and digital work. Kate creates images that are soft and organic, and ones that are hard and rectilinear. Kate would like her live/create environment to reflect these dichotic sides of herself and her work.

Kate's aesthetic preferences are as dichotic as her personality. She values natural, flowing, botanical, curvilinear forms; rustic and weathered materials; an industrial style with hard edges and hard materials; subdued natural colours; and bright vivid colours.

Table A01 End user profiles, needs and activities

	Values	Personality	Psychological Needs	Future Needs	Activities
Primary end user					
Kate	Freedom Creativity Spontaneity Honesty Order	Extraverted Open-minded Intuitive Independent Creative	Control Security Variety	Mobility scooter	Prepare meals Eat/dine[3] Entertain Watch TV Listen to music Read Sleep Personal hygiene House clean Laundry Cat care Draw, paint, airbrush Digital graphic work Research Scooter maintenance Pay bills
Ash (the cat)	Food	Sweet	Options Views Security	Stairs to get up to Kate's bed	Eat, sleep Play Get groomed Use litter box
Future partner	Unknown	Unknown	Unknown	Unknown	Unknown
Secondary end user					
Family, friends and guests	Wide range	Varied	Comfort Wayfinding	N/A	Prepare meals[2] Eat/dine[3] Socialize Watch TV, Read Nap[4] Sleep Personal hygiene Scooter maintenance[5] Pack/unpack Sketch[6]
Tertiary end user					
Other[1]	N/A	N/A	Wayfinding	N/A	Deliver Repair

Notes
[1] Courier, work supplies deliveries, maintenance workers.
[2] Close friends and family may help with meal preparation and clean up.
[3] Eating is informal; dining is formal.
[4] Secondary end users may take naps depending on the length of their stay.
[5] Kate and some of her friends often get together to work on their scooters.
[6] Kate and some clients sketch ideas for airbrushing.

Activity Summary

A detailed analysis of Kate's day-to-day activities led to the following conclusions:

- Kate spends almost half of her time doing "living" related activities (11 hours)
- Kate spends the rest of her time doing graphic design and airbrush work, and leisure activities outside of her live space (12 hours)
- On weekends, Kate spends anywhere from 12–18 hours doing living activities, and 6–12 hours doing leisure activities including working on her scooters, entertaining friends, riding her scooter, drawing, reading, or listening to music

Further analyses of Kate's activities, secondary end user activities, and mechanical requirements led to the conclusion that there should be seven zones within the three-story building including a:

1. Live Zone (semi-private).
2. Create Zone 1 (private).
3. Create Zone 2 (private).
4. Grey Zone (private).
5. Entertain Zone (semi-private).
6. Scooter Zone (semi-private).
7. Mechanical Zone.

It is apparent that Kate's daily routine has her moving back-and-forth from her Live Zone to all of the other zones. To minimize circulation, Kate's Live Zone should be central to the other zones. This finding contradicts one of the assumptions stated at the beginning of the program (that the Live Zone would be on the third floor). An additional noteworthy finding was that each zone should have a distinct degree of privacy that is either private or semi-private.

Spatial Requirements

Live Zone

Table A02 Live Zone spatial requirements

Activity	# People Involved	Item	#	Dimensions L W H mm	Notes
Meal preparation	1–3	Refrigerator	1	887 600 3064	Gas hob
		Hob	1	650 510 57	
		Cooker hood	1	898 500 60/1150	Client is willing to
		Built-in oven	1	594 568 589	have a cooker if
		Microwave	1	595 560 455	a hob and built-
		Undercounter dishwasher	1	597 555 820 840 460	in oven are not possible.
		Undermount double sink	3	600-900 660 Standard upper and lower cabinets	
		Prep counter	10		
		Storage for:	10		
		baking pans & racks	6		Whenever
		pots & pans	20		possible, all
		mixing bowls	60		lower kitchen
		serve ware	40		cabinets should
		dishware	20		be drawers
		flatware	48		
		utensils	24		
		glassware			
		drinkware			All kitchen
		dry goods			cabinets to
		spices	1	490 600 670	have soft-close
		canned goods	2	TBD	hardware
		*All-in-one espresso maker			
		Seating			Meal prep seating should be stools
Eat/dine	1–6	*Antique table	1	1200 2000 80	
		*Seating	6	450 500 1010	
Watch TV	1–4	*65" smart tv	1	1450.1 39.9 831.2	Full articulating wall mount for tv
		Soft seating	TBD		Seating must accommodate laying down
Listen to music	1–4	Network amplifier	1	380 380 91	Bookshelf
		Floor speakers	2	351 450 1050	speakers to be
		Bookshelf speakers	2	192 256 327	wall-mounted
		Soft seating	1	TBD	
		Side table	1	TBD	

(continued)

Table A02 (Cont.)

Activity	# People Involved	Item	#	Dimensions L W H mm	Notes
Read Nap	1	Soft seating/lounging	1	1170 1070 640	
Exercise	1	Yoga mat Weights Misc. equip		Open or closed shelving storage	
Sleep	1–2	*King size bed Night table Folded clothes storage Hanging clothes storage seating	1 2 1	1610 2300 1140 TBD Closed storage 1828–3657 TBD	
Personal hygiene	1–2	Toilet Washbasin Shower Soaking tub Storage for towels and personal items	1 1 1 1	Standard 1219 min. Standard Standard Closed storage	Shower and tub can be all-in-one
House clean	1	Storage for cleaning supplies, rags, broom mop, vacuum, buckets, etc.		As needed	
Laundry	1	Washer Dryer Ironing board Storage for detergent, etc. Hanging storage	1 1 1	Standard Standard Wall hung Shelving 1219 +/-	
Cat care	1	Dry and wet food storage Food & water bowls Cat scratcher Cat bed Toy storage Litter Box Grooming equipment	2 2 1 1 1 1 1	As needed	

* Existing FFE to be re-used.
TBD = To be determined (designer to select in consultation with client).

Create Zone 1

Table A03 Create Zone 1 spatial requirements

Activity	# People	Item	#	Dimensions L W H mm	Notes
Digital graphic work	1–3	Table	1	1828 762 812	Self-healing surface
		Desk	1	TBD	
		Task chair	1	TBD	
		Side chair	2	TBD	
		*Monitors	2	Table top	
		*Computer	2	Table top	
		*Printer	1	1268 696 913	
		*Scanner	1	TBD	
		Misc. computer hardware		As needed	
		File storage	1	TBD	
Read	1	Soft seating	1	TBD	
		Side table	1	TBD	
Listen to music	1	Bookshelf speakers	2	192 256 327	Bookshelf speakers to be wall-mounted
Personal hygiene	1	Toilet	1	Standard	
		Washbasin	1	Standard	

* Existing FFE to be re-used.
TBD = To be determined (designer to select in consultation with client).

Create Zone 2

Table A04 Create Zone 2 spatial requirements

Activity	# People	Item	#	Dimensions L W H mm	Notes
Airbrush work	1–3	Work surface	TBD	6096 min.	Could be counters or tables
		Stool	3	TBD	
		Storage (paint, etc.)	As needed		
Paint	1	*Antique	1	5995 5792 1719	1 table to be mobile
		Easel	2	TBD	
		Stool	2	1219 762 812	
		Table	As needed	Open & closed shelving	
		Storage for paper, canvas, paint, brushes, etc.			

(*continued*)

Table A04 (Cont.)

Activity	# People	Item	#	Dimensions L W H mm	Notes

Listen to music
Read
Become inspired
	1	Bookshelf
		    speakers
		Soft seating
		Side table
			1
			1
			1
				192 256 327
				TBD
				TBD
					Bookshelf
					    speakers to be
					    wall-mounted

Personal hygiene	1	Toilet Washbasin	1 1	Standard Standard	

* Existing FFE to be re-used.
TBD = To be determined (designer to select in consultation with client).

Grey Zone

Table A05 Grey Zone spatial requirements

Activity	# People	Item	#	Dimensions L W H mm	Notes
Draw	1	Soft seat Mobile side table	1 1	TBD TBD	
Meditate	1	Soft floor cushion	1	TBD	

Listen to music
Read
Become inspired
	1	Bookshelf
		    speakers
		Soft seating
		Side table
			1
			1
			1
				192 256 327
				TBD
				TBD
					Bookshelf speakers to
					    be wall-mounted

Personal hygiene	1	Toilet Washbasin	1 1	Standard Standard	

* Existing FFE to be re-used.
TBD = To be determined (designer to select in consultation with client).

Entertain Zone

Table A06 Entertain Zone spatial requirements

Activity	# People	Item	#	Dimensions L W H mm	Notes
Food and beverage Prep.	2–8	Refrigerator Coffee machine Kettle Storage (glassware, cutlery, condiments, snacks, etc.) Prep. counter Sink (1.5 bowl) Microwave	1 1 1 8 1 1 1	Full size Counter top Counter top Open or closed as needed Standard counter TBD Shelf mount	All cabinets and drawers to have soft close hardware.
Watch TV Listen to music Nap Read	1–8	65" smart tv Soft seating for 8 Side tables Floor speakers Bookshelf speakers	1 TBD 2–3 2 2	1450.1 39.9 831.2 TBD 351 450 1050 192 256 327	Full articulating wall mount for tv Seating must accommodate laying down Bookshelf speakers to be wall-mounted
Overnight guests	1–2	King bed Night stand Chair Luggage valet Hanging storage Clothes storage TV	1 2 1 1 TBD 1	1610 2300 1140 TBD TBD TBD 1219 +/- As needed 300 300	Wall mounted
Personal hygiene	1–8	Toilet Washbasin Walk-in shower Storage for towels and personal items	1 1 1 1	Standard 1219 min. Standard Closed storage	

TBD = To be determined (designer to select in consultation with client).

Scooter Zone

Table A07 Scooter Zone spatial requirements

Activity	# People	Item	#	Dimensions L W H mm	Notes
Scooter maintenance	1–3	Seating	3	TBD	
		Work bench	2	1828 min	
		Open shelving	As needed	3656 min	
		Tool storage	As needed	TBD	
		Hydraulic scooter lift	1		
Listen to music	1–3	Bookshelf speakers	1	192 256 327	Bookshelf speakers to be wall-mounted
Personal hygiene	1–3	Toilet	1	Standard	
		Washbasin	1	Standard	

* Existing FFE to be re-used.
TBD = To be determined (designer to select in consultation with client).

Mechanical Zone

Table A08 Mechanical Zone spatial requirements

Activity	# People	Item	#	Dimensions L W H mm	Notes
N/A	N/A	Electrical panel	1	As needed	70kVA
N/A	N/A	Heat source	1	As needed	Client prefers energy efficient mechanical systems
N/A	N/A	Air conditioning system	1	As needed	Condenser to be located at rear of property (lane side)
N/A	N/A	Hot water source	1	As needed	
N/A	N/A	City water source	1	As needed	
N/A	N/A	Grey water collection	1	As needed	
N/A	N/A	City drain source	1	As needed	

* Existing FFE to be re-used.
TBD = To be determined (designer to select in consultation with client).

Area Requirements

CREATE 1
37.05 m^2

GREY
37.05 m^2

SCOOTER
88.92 m^2

LIVE
148.20 m^2

ENTERTAIN
111.15 m^2

CREATE 2
27.93 m^2

MECH.
22.23 m^2

TOTAL: *423.53 m^2
*circulation is included in each zone

Figure A06 Area requirements

Spatial Adjacencies

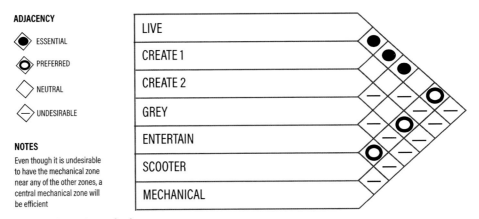

ADJACENCY

◉ ESSENTIAL

◎ PREFERRED

◇ NEUTRAL

⬦ UNDESIRABLE

NOTES

Even though it is undesirable
to have the mechanical zone
near any of the other zones, a
central mechanical zone will
be efficient

LIVE	
CREATE 1	
CREATE 2	
GREY	
ENTERTAIN	
SCOOTER	
MECHANICAL	

Figure A07 Spatial adjacency matrix

Zoning and Circulation

Analysis led to the conclusion that the ground floor would house the Create Zone 2, Entertain Zone, Scooter Zone, and Mechanical Zone. The second level would be the Live Zone, and the third level would be part Create Zone 1, Grey Zone, and Live Zone.

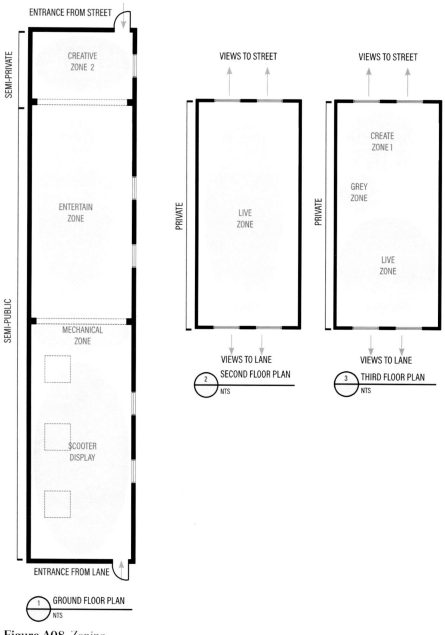

Figure A08 Zoning

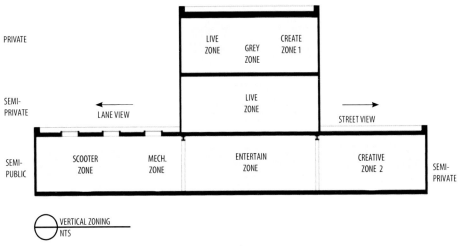

PRIVATE

LIVE ZONE   GREY ZONE   CREATE ZONE 1

SEMI-PRIVATE

LANE VIEW ←

LIVE ZONE

STREET VIEW →

SEMI-PUBLIC

SCOOTER ZONE   MECH. ZONE   ENTERTAIN ZONE   CREATIVE ZONE 2

SEMI-PRIVATE

VERTICAL ZONING
NTS

Figure A09 Stacking diagram (vertical zoning)

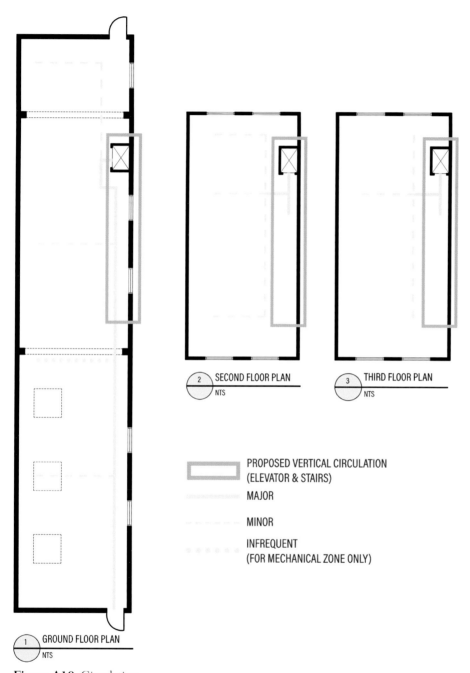

2 — SECOND FLOOR PLAN
NTS

3 — THIRD FLOOR PLAN
NTS

PROPOSED VERTICAL CIRCULATION
(ELEVATOR & STAIRS)

MAJOR

MINOR

INFREQUENT
(FOR MECHANICAL ZONE ONLY)

1 — GROUND FLOOR PLAN
NTS

Figure A10 Circulation

Design Guidelines

Issue: Contrast

>   Objective: Each zone should have an aesthetic that reflects one of Kate's dichotic personalities – linear and hard, slightly industrial; soft and flowing, slightly feminine; and a combination industrial and feminine.
>
>   >   Concept: Consider creating a "spatial identity" for each zone using distinct form, colour, and pattern.
>   >
>   >   Concept: Consider providing lighting controls in each zone so that different moods can be created.

Issue: Inspiration

>   Objective: With the exception of the Mechanical Zone, all zones should stimulate Kate's creativity as much as possible.
>
>   >   Concept: In the create zones, consider maximizing street views since Kate finds the local street activity to be inspiring.
>   >
>   >   Concept: Consider installing adjustable shelving and a flexible display system that Kate can use to display an ever-changing collection of inspirational images and objects.
>   >
>   >   Concept: Consider developing a rooftop outdoor area with access from Kate's Live Zone and from the Entertainment Zone.

Issue: Security

>   Objective: Kate should feel secure in her large three-story building.
>
>   >   Concept: Consider installing a full security system that will allow Kate to monitor activity on all three levels and outside her building.
>   >
>   >   Concept: Consider creating a multi-zone control centre where Kate can control and monitor the security system along with the music and HVAC systems.

Issue: Privacy

>   Objective: Kate's Live, Create, and Grey Zones should be private and semi-private areas.

Concept: Consider installing lockable doors and a card lock elevator between Kate's semi-private zones and semi-public zones such as the entertainment and scooter zones.

Concept: Consider installing window coverings or special glass coatings that will allow Kate to view out but restrict views in.

Schematic Perspectives

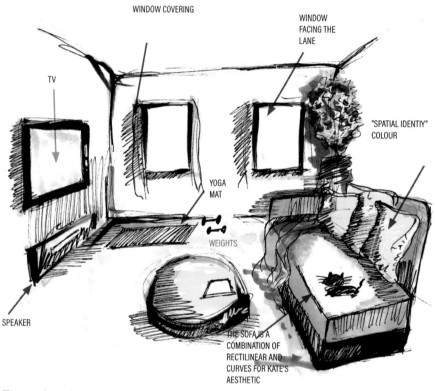

Figure A11 Live Zone

ADJUSTABLE SHELVING AND A
FLEXIBLE DISPLAY SYSTEM

MULTI-ZONE CONTROL AREA
(SECURITY SYSTEM, MUSIC, AND
HVAC SYSTEMS)

Figure A12 Create Zone 1

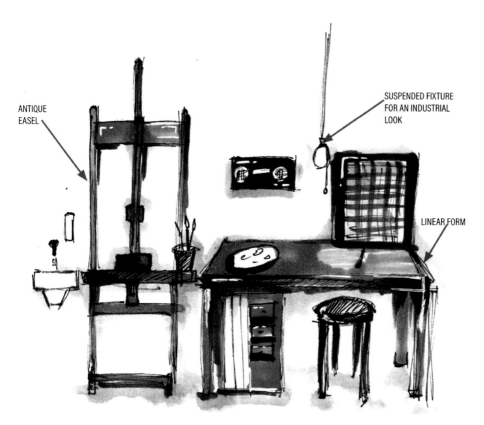

ANTIQUE EASEL

SUSPENDED FIXTURE FOR AN INDUSTRIAL LOOK

LINEAR FORM

Figure A13 Create Zone 2

Figure A14 Grey Zone

APPENDIX B

Figure B01 *The Hub Program*, South Central Canada (unless noted, all Appendix B figures by Shane Cuenca; all Appendix B tables by author)

TABLE OF CONTENTS

THE HUB PROGRAM

Overview

A rural municipality (RM) owns a large acreage in south central Canada. During the spring, summer, and fall months the property is used for motorsport events such as motorcycle, dirt bike, sports car, and drag racing; (go)karting; and all-terrain vehicle riding. To accommodate the needs of the people who attend these events, the RM would like to renovate an old barn that exists on its property. The barn would become a hub for various activities such as driving schools, driver/rider meetings, awards presentations, and year-end banquets. The barn would also include a concession stand and small bar.

The RM sees the barn renovation project as the first of many projects in a long-term development plan that will eventually include a restaurant/bar, motel, camping facilities, outdoor activity areas, and upgraded racing facilities. The intent is to develop a facility that can operate year-round and attract not just motor sport enthusiasts, but cross-country skiers and snowmobilers in the winter months, tourists during the summer, and locals all year round. The client envisions the entire development as an event space for conferences, weddings, and other events. In addition, with upgraded racing facilities, the RM would be eligible to host national race events numerous times a year thereby attracting large numbers of spectators.

Objectives

- To create a casual atmosphere that would appeal to a large number of end users
- To act as a transition between outdoors and indoors
- To create space that fosters enthusiasm for outdoor activities whether the activities are passive, adventurous, or competitive
- To create a welcoming atmosphere for tourists
- To create a flexible space that can be configured many different ways and serve many different needs
- To create an environment that reflects the character of the facility's location

Assumptions

- That the concession will be open all year round (implies access from inside and outside)
- That an addition will be added to the barn to accommodate mechanical equipment, the bar, and the concession
- That new mechanical, electrical, and plumbing systems will be installed
- That the structure may require repairs
- That the entire facility, including the loft, will be accessible

Occupant Profiles, Activities, and Needs

Occupancy Type and Load

According to the "International Building Code" (as cited by Harmon and Kennon, 2014, 65), the HUB is classified as an A-2 Assembly occupancy with food and beverage consumption. The occupant load would be 150 (Harmon and Kennon, 2014, 101).

Source: Harmon, Sharon K. and Katherine E. Kennon. 2014. *The Codes Guidebook for Interiors*. 6th ed. Hoboken, NJ: Wiley.

Primary Occupants

Primary and secondary occupants will include individuals of all genders and ages.

Tertiary end users could be any gender but will likely be aged 16+.

Table B01 Primary occupant profiles, activities, and needs

Primary activities	# participants	Characteristics	Activities	Needs/special needs
Enthusiasts of **passive** outdoor activities	1–100	Family-oriented Health-conscious Nature lover	Cross country skiing, snowmobiling, hiking, bicycle riding Socializing Eating Watching movies Playing games	Washroom Storage locker Mud room with hose Change room Place to eat (indoor & outdoor) Cd player/USB Projector Screen Lounge table and seating for game playing Fireplace

(continued)

Table B01 (Cont.)

Primary activities	# participants	Characteristics	Activities	Needs/special needs
Enthusiasts of **adventurous** outdoor activities	1–100	Adventuresome Outgoing Daring	Dirt bike, ATV[1] & UTV[2] trail & bog riding; hill climbing Socializing Eating Rider meetings Amateur contests Watching movies Playing games Awards Year-end banquet	Same as above + Seating for rider meetings Bulletin board to post notifications, classifieds, etc. Podium Track/bog maps projected onto screen
Enthusiasts of **competitive** outdoor activities	1–100	Athletic Competitive	Dirt bike, road, drag, car, kart racing; hill climbing Socializing Eating Rider meetings Race schools Watching movies Playing games Awards Year-end banquet	Same as above + Tables or desks Large screen tv 4 medium screen TVs
Attendees at events such as: weddings, anniversaries, retirement or birthday parties, holiday celebrations, family reunions, music concerts, bingo), conferences, retreats, arts and crafts shows, farmers markets	40–150	Wide variety	Socializing Eating Presentations/speeches Ceremonies Watching videos/ slideshows Games Break out groups, discussions Learning Dancing	Seating for 125 people Tables for 125 people Podium Lectern Stage for DJ with **plenty of electrical outlets** Music/PA announcement system for the entire facility CD player & USB receiver Projector Screen Lounge table and seating for game playing Dance floor Fireplace
Employees[3]	3–6	Cheerful	Preparing food Serving beverages Cleaning up	Lockable storage Staff room or equiv.
Volunteers[4]	8–30	Friendly	Relaxing, socializing	Lockable storage

Notes:
1 ATV = All-terrain vehicle.
2 UTV = Utility vehicle or side-by-side.
3 Concession, bar employees (maintenance and grounds keeping to be provided by the RM).
4 Timekeepers, corner workers, marshals, referees, etc.

Secondary Occupants

Table B02 Secondary occupant profiles, activities, and needs

	# participants	Characteristics	Activities	Needs/special needs
Spectators	1–300	Adventuresome Competitive Dynamic Energized Family-oriented	Spectating Socializing Eating Walking Riding bicycles	Washroom Place to eat (indoor & outdoor) CD player/USB Projector Screen Lounge table and seating for game playing Fireplace
Emergency Medical Responders (EMR)	2–4	Focused Professional	Working Eating Attending to injured people	Washroom Place to eat
Tourists	1–60	Curious Adventuresome Energized Passive	Spectating Camping Socializing Eating Relaxing Walking Riding bicycles	Washroom Place to eat (indoor & outdoor) CD player/USB Projector Screen Lounge table and seating for game playing Fireplace

Tertiary Occupants

Table B03 Tertiary occupant profiles, activities, and needs

	# Participants	Characteristics	Activities	Needs/special needs
Media personalities	1–6	Outgoing Curious Professional	Documenting activities Announcing live activities Conducting interviews Taking photos	Announcement desk Computer or laptop Desk seating PA equipment
Food/alcohol deliveries	1–2	Professional	Delivering food or alcohol	Loading area
DJs and performers	1–6	Artistic Creative	DJing Playing music Performing	Loading area Stage Seating Coat storage Lots of electrical outlets Washroom

Summary

Based on the project objectives and end user analysis, *The HUB* will include five activity zones:

1. Entry zone (including washrooms, change rooms, showers, mud rinse area, secure lockers)
2. Social zone (including stage, furniture and equipment storage, secure electronic equipment area)
3. Food zone (including the concession)
4. Drink zone (including the bar)
5. Support zone (including mechanical space, janitorial area, employee staff room, employee washroom)

Activity Zone Furniture, Fixtures, and Equipment

Entry Zone

The actitivity zone should be bright and welcoming. Entry zone activities include: entering/exiting; waiting; removing/putting on outerwear; using washroom, change room, or shower; conversing; viewing bulletin board; warming up or cooling down.

Table B04 Entry zone furniture, fixtures, and equipment

Item	Quantity and/or dimensions	Notes
General seating & seating for gear removal	4–8	Should be highly durable and able to withstand wet conditions
Seating lockers	20–30	To store helmets, gloves, jackets, pants, or other gear. Gear may be wet or muddy
General coat storage	9–12 linear feet	Coats may be wet
Helmet/boot/ hand wear dryer	2	
Washrooms	Female: 2 w/c 1 accessible w/c 2 lavatory 1 accessible lavatory Male: Same as above	The client has also requested an accessible unisex employee w/c and lavatory
Hand sanitizer	1	
Garbage & recycling containers	1 each	
Digital and traditional announcement boards	1 of each Max size 4' x 4'	

Social Zone

The social zone should be open and visually interesting (perhaps using the barn structure, loft, or fireplace as a focal point). The zone should encourage conversation, and should appeal to a wide range of aesthetic preferences.

Social zone activities include: socializing, learning, meeting, awards ceremonies, banquets, informal eating, formal dining, consuming alcohol, playing games, watching videos, dancing, listening to music, conferences, retreats, group work/discussions, live bands, arts and crafts sales, bingos, etc.

Table B05 Social zone furniture, fixtures, and equipment

Item	Quantity and/or Dimensions	Notes
Lounge seating	20–30	
Conference seating	125	
Lounge tables	12	For food, beverages, etc.
Work tables	To accommodate 125 people	Must have the ability to be configured a variety of different ways
Stage	1	For DJ or live band
3 tier podium	1	Must be on casters
Gas fireplace	1	
Storage for seating, work and lounge tables, podium, lectern, bingo machine,		Must accommodate 70 chairs, work tables, podium, and other furniture and equipment
Media screen	1	Placed where maximum number of people can see it
Ceiling mounted projector	1	
Stereo amplifier	1	
Wall mounted speakers	8–12	
Televisions	4–6	
Garbage & recycling containers	8–12 of each	

Food Zone

The food zone will serve customers from both inside and outside *The HUB*. Having the food zone open to the interior will allow the facilities to be used for weddings, retirement parties, or any other event where special food (not concession food) is required. Essential to the food zone are a secure employee area, delivery door, and access to outdoor garbage and recycling bins.

Food zone activities include: receiving deliveries, storing food, preparing food, taking orders, serving food, placing orders for supplies, washing dishes, removing garbage.

Table B06 Food zone furniture, fixtures, and equipment

Item	Quantity and/or Dimensions	Notes
Glass door, reach-in refrigerator (condiments, eggs, butter, milk, sandwich fillings, vegetables, fish, cheese, sour cream, creamers, yogurt)	1 54"x32"x84"	
Glass door, reach-in freezer storage (fries, hamburgers, hot dogs, smokies, ice cream, gelato, etc.)	1 54"x32"x84"	
Single glass door beverage merchandiser	1 27"x32"x84	
Range with griddle	1 60"x33"x60"	
Dual basket deep fryer (floor type)	1 16"x30"x46"	
Microwave oven	1 23"x20"x14"	
Coffee brewer with 3 warmers and hot water dispenser	1 16"x18"x18"	
4 slice bread & bagel toaster	1 12"x9"x9"	
Pastry display	18"x17.8"x16.3"	
Snack display	22"x21"x11"	

Table B06 *(Cont.)*

Item	Quantity and/or Dimensions	Notes
Vegetable prep. table	4–6'	
Meat prep table	4'	
General work table	4–6	
Order taking & serving counter with cash register	2 3–4 each	
Serving ware storage (plates, take out containers, cutlery, cups, napkins)	5 linear ft. open shelving	
Dry goods storage (bread, coffee, tea, hot, chocolate, sugar, potato chips, pastry, seasonings)	5 linear ft. open shelving	
Pots and pans storage		Pots can be hung above prep. and work tables, or stored beneath the same tables
Utensils storage (knives, ladles, flippers, tongs, etc.)	Wall mounted &/or counter top storage	
3 compartment sink with drainboard	1 66.5"x20.5"x45"	
Dishwasher	1 30"x29"x68"	
Wall-mounted hand wash sink with soap & paper towel dispensers	1 17"x15"x26"	
26 gallon slim garbage & recycling containers	4 22"x14"x32"	

Drink Zone

The drink zone will serve customers from inside *The HUB* only. Although small, this zone will contain everything needed to support *The HUB* activities. Drink zone activities include: receiving deliveries, storing alcohol, taking orders, serving alcohol (counter service only, cleaning up, and removing garbage).

Table B07 Drink zone furniture, fixtures, and equipment

Item	Quantity	
2–3 door back bar cooler (beer)	1 48/72"x25"x36"	
1–2 door back bar cooler (wine, coolers, misc. garnishes)	3 24/48"x25"x36"	
6-button soda gun with 6 soda canisters (undercounter)	1 72" wide x 48" high	
Counter top blender	1 9"x9.5"x21"	
Single underbar sink with drainboard	1 24"x19"x33"	
Undercounter dishwasher	1 24"x25"x33"	
Single countertop coffee maker	1 8.25"x17.75"x19"	
Liquor display	3 tiers 4–6 linear ft. each	
Drinkware storage (tall, short, beer, wine glasses, coffee cups)	8 linear ft. open shelving	Can be suspended over serving area
2 level service counter	4–6 linear ft. x 48" H	
Dry goods storage (nuts, napkins, coasters, stir sticks, sugar)	6–9 linear ft.	
Drink mixing utensil storage (knives, shot glasses, towels, shakers)	2 standard drawers 2' wide x 6" high 2–3 linear ft.	
Garbage & recycling	1 of each	

Support Zone

Table B08 Support zone furniture, fixtures, and equipment

Item	Quantity &/or Dimensions	Notes
HVAC equipment	As required	
Hot water tank	1	
Electrical panel	1	
Storage for mops, brooms, buckets, vacuum	As required	Mops, etc. can be hung on wall
Storage for cleaning & washroom supplies	12' open shelving	
Floor sink	1	

Area Requirements

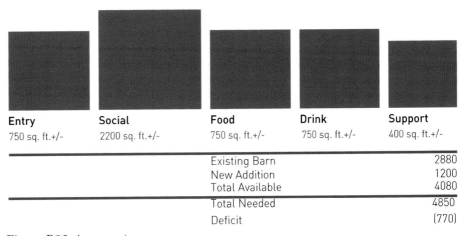

Entry	Social	Food	Drink	Support
750 sq. ft.+/–	2200 sq. ft.+/–	750 sq. ft.+/–	750 sq. ft.+/–	400 sq. ft.+/–

Existing Barn	2880
New Addition	1200
Total Available	4080
Total Needed	4850
Deficit	(770)

Figure B02 Area requirements

Site

The large acre parcel of land for the client's long-term development plan sits between two major highways (on the east and west sides), and two minor highways (on the north and south sides). The site is surrounded by prairie grasses and unobstructed vistas. A large body of water is located to the west of the site. Strong winds are a common occurrence in the open prairie landscape.

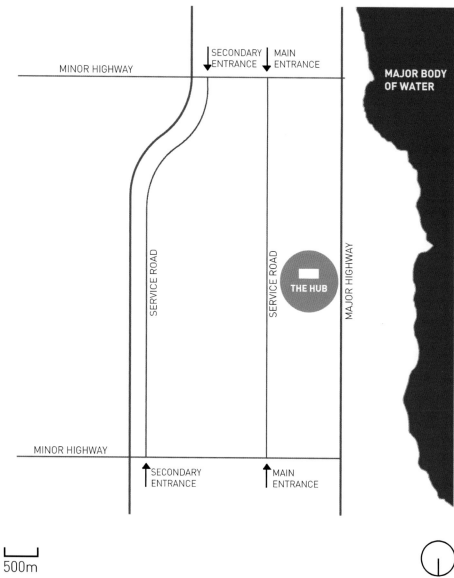

Figure B03 Site plan

Opportunities

- The relatively flat site provides numerous opportunities for future additions to, or extensions of *The HUB*

- The flat prairie landscape provides beautiful vistas
- There is plenty of opportunity for parking all kinds of vehicles including recreational vehicles such as snowmobiles, ATVs, and quads

Constraints
- Open landscape provides little protection from the elements especially wind

Building

Built in the early 1900s, the barn was constructed of fir beams from BC, and logs from a nearby townsite. Vacant since 1976, the time-worn building will require an almost complete re-build, but the RM believes that the character of the structure is well worth preserving. The barn has approximately 2880 square feet of interior space.

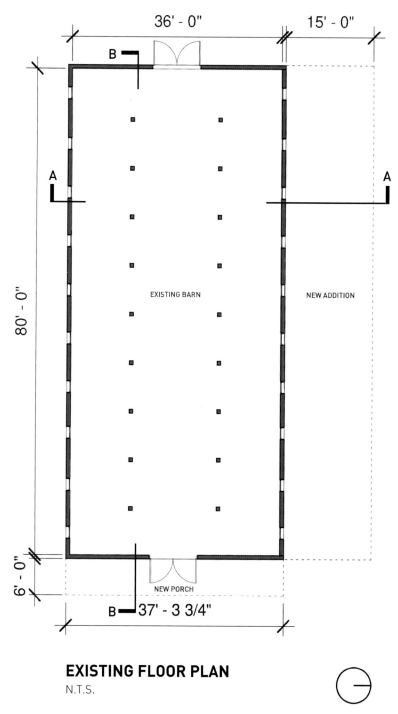

EXISTING FLOOR PLAN
N.T.S.

Figure B04 Building plan

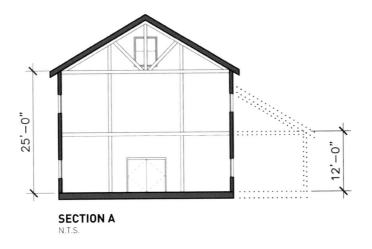

SECTION A
N.T.S.

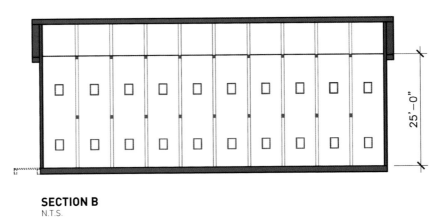

SECTION B
N.T.S.

Figure B05 Building sections

Opportunities

- An open interior space, with evenly-spaced columns, provides plenty of space for social activities, and for relatively unimpeded planning
- The character of the existing structure and aged timber reflects the barn's age and geographic location; features worth retaining

Constraints

- The barn requires a complete retrofit including building envelope, floor, and mechanical systems

Spatial Adjacencies

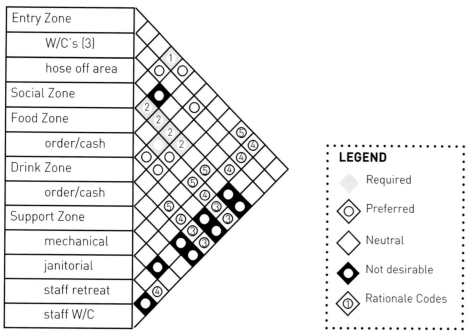

Figure B06 Spatial adjacencies

Rationale

1 Occupants will use social zone more frequently than other zones
2 Easier for occupants to pick up food and drink in one location
3 Provides employees easy access to retreat and W/C
4 These zones and activities will need frequent janitorial services
5 A centralized mechanical area will be more efficient than one that is not centralized

Zoning and Circulation

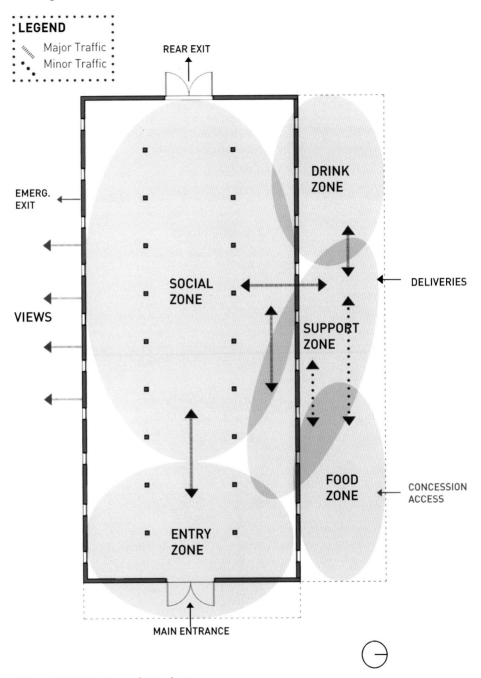

Figure B07 Zoning and circulation

Design Guidelines

Issue: Flexibility

    Objective: The social space should be as open as possible, and have as little fixed or built-in furniture as possible, in order to accommodate multiple furniture arrangements

        Concept: Consider using stacking chairs and folding tables that can be stored when not in use

        Concept: Consider using lounge seating with casters

        Concept: Consider using stackable side tables

    Objective: End users should be able to control lighting in order to create a variety of moods

        Concept: Consider having lighting on dimmers

        Concept: Consider having remote controlled window coverings

Issue: Image/atmosphere

    Objective: *The HUB* should have a welcoming atmosphere that appeals to a wide range of end users

        Concept: Consider incorporating a neutral décor, simple forms, and minimal ornamentation

    Objective: *The HUB* should have a casual atmosphere

        Concept: Consider using natural and/or local materials

        Concept: Consider using unpretentious materials and finishes

Issue: Durability

    Objective: *The HUB* and its furnishings should be able to withstand mud, snow, and water

        Concept: Consider installing waterproof materials where ever possible

Conceptual Drawings

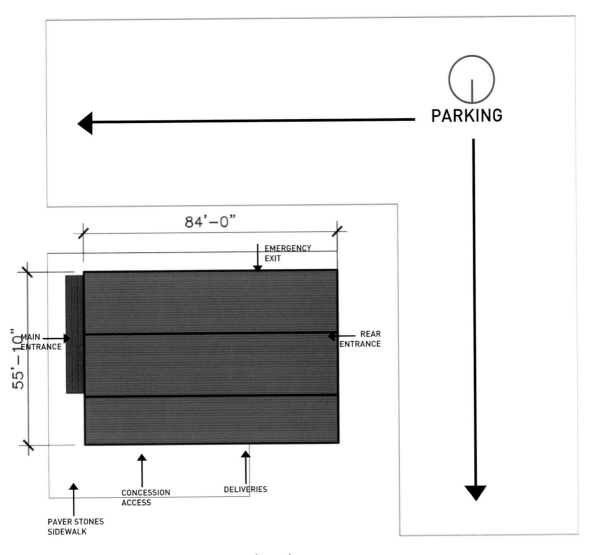

Figure B08 Conceptual site plan

CONCESSION
ACCESS

DELIVERIES

Figure B09 Conceptual north elevation

Figure B10 Conceptual west elevation

APPENDIX C

Figure C01 *Extreme Toy Hauler Mobile Showroom Program*, USA (unless noted, all Appendix C figures by Josh Lingal; all Appendix C tables by author)

TABLE OF CONTENTS

EXECUTIVE SUMMARY

Extreme Toy Hauler (ETH) is a company that specializes in a particular segment of the recreational vehicles (RV) market – toy haulers. With the aim of becoming the number one choice for customized toy haulers across the US, ETH has commissioned this program for three toy hauler mobile showrooms.

Travelling to a variety of events and exhibitions across the US, these showrooms will provide customers with an immersive retail experience in which customers can design their very own toy haulers using design technology such as augmented and virtual reality.

Mobile Showroom Goals and Objectives

Goals

- To provide customers with an exceptional retail experience
- To provide employees with an exceptional work experience
- To educate customers about ETH's toy hauler design, innovations, function, and amenities
- To increase the company's profile and generate more sales

Objectives

- Create an **immersive retail experience** for customers
- Provide showrooms in which employees and customers can **work, learn, relax,** and be **entertained**
- Design showrooms that reflect the **high-quality materials and crafts-manship** used in ETH's toy haulers
- Design showrooms that will **appeal to toy hauler enthusiasts with different needs and lifestyles**
- Project a **strong brand presence** at each event, exhibition, or trade show

Toy Haulers

Extreme Toy Hauler has determined that a flexible solution, consisting of three mobile showroom sizes (small, medium, large), along with an employee support and a lavatorial toy hauler, will enable ETH to fit in at almost any event anywhere in the US.

Small Travel Trailer
> 21' long | 8' wide | 8' ceiling height | 202 ft^2
> 3–4 sellers
> 2–3 customers

Large Fifth Wheel
> 41' long | 8'-6" wide | 8'-6" ceiling height | 417 ft^2
> 4–6 sellers
> 1–8 customers

Class A
> 39'-9" long | 8' wide | 8' ceiling height | 386 ft^2
> 6–8 sellers
> 1–12 customers

Employee Support
> 38' long | 8' wide | 8' ceiling height | 375 ft^2
> 6–8 sellers and/or drivers

Lavatorial
> 39'-9" long | 8' wide | 8' ceiling height | 386 ft^2
> One men's washroom, one women's washroom, and one family washroom
> Separate storage space for toiletries and cleaning supplies

Site Configuration Options

Although ETH will be able to configure any number and type of showrooms to suit each occasion and site, three sample configurations are described below.

The Strip

5,352 ft^2

Two large fifth wheel, employee support, and lavatorial toy haulers

The Square

13,820 ft^2

Small travel trailer, employee support, and lavatorial toy haulers

The U-Shape

20,300 ft^2

Three large fifth wheel, three small travel trailer, two class A, employee support, and lavatorial toy haulers

Design Guidelines

Based on ETH's goals and the project objectives, the following issues were identified as being essential for the success of the project:

Innovation

Craftsmanship

Brand Identity

Immersive Retail Experience

EXTREME TOY HAULER MOBILE SHOWROOM PROGRAM

Extreme Toyhauler Overview

A US company called Extreme Toy Haulers (ETH) recently built a recreational vehicle (RV) super center that caters exclusively to toy hauler enthusiasts. The *Extreme Toy Hauler Super Centre* provides customers with an immersive retail experience by having customers use augmented reality (AR) and virtual reality (VR) to design custom toy haulers. The toy haulers are then built, on site, with pre-fabricated components.

Inspired by high end automobile companies (that have developed mobile showrooms for particular vehicles), ETH now wants to develop a mobile show-room. Once designed, several of the showrooms will travel across the country to different events, exhibitions, and trade shows. ETH believes that bringing their product directly to customers will increase sales exponentially.

Like the *Extreme Toy Hauler Super Centre*, the mobile showrooms will incorporate AR and VR with the intention being to provide customers with an immersive retail experience.

Company Profile

ETH is an eight-year-old company that was established to meet the needs of toy hauler enthusiasts. The company employs over 1,000 people and, last year, achieved over 80 billion dollars in sales.

The company retails high end toy haulers that provide living quarters and storage for almost any type of "toy" including motorcycles, quads, bicycles, kayaks, and other recreational equipment. Toy haulers range in size from small to large, and include non-motorized and motorized versions.

ETH attracts wealthy customers who expect the best in terms of toy hauler function, form, and finish. Regardless of size, each toy hauler includes innovative technologies, high-end products and finishes, and extreme craftsmanship.

Vision

To become the number one choice for toy hauler customers in the US.

Mission

To provide exceptional customer and employee experiences.

Core Values

Innovation

Craftsmanship

Loyalty

Business Objectives

To provide innovative and well-crafted toy hauler products and services not available anywhere else in the US.

To develop life-long customers.

To attract and retain highly qualified employees.

To provide customers with an immersive and integrated retail experience (where employees and customers interact).

To have a toy hauler super centre in all major cities across the US.

Organizational Structure

Extreme Toy Haulers has a pyramid-shaped organizational structure in which all parts of the structure support one main element – retail.

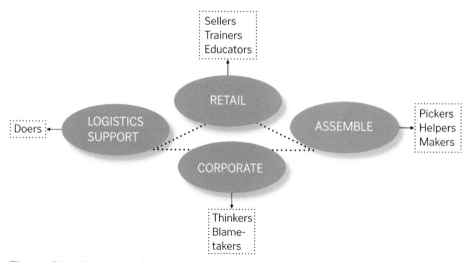

Figure C02 Extreme toy hauler organizational structure

Mobile Showroom Goals, Objectives, and Operational Assumptions

Goals

- To provide customers with an exceptional retail experience
- To provide employees with an exceptional work experience
- To educate customers about ETH's toy hauler design, innovations, function, and amenities
- To increase the company's profile and generate more sales

Objectives

The following objectives consider the project goals as well as the results of the literature analysis. Developed in conjunction with ETH representatives, these objectives define the intended essence of end design product.

- Create an **immersive retail experience** for customers
- Provide showrooms in which employees and customers can **work, learn, relax,** and be **entertained**
- Design showrooms that reflect the **high-quality materials and craftsmanship** used in ETH's toy haulers
- Design showrooms that will **appeal to toy hauler enthusiasts with different needs and lifestyles**
- Project a **strong brand presence** at each event, exhibition, or trade show

Operational Assumptions

ETH envisions their mobile showrooms and "sellers" (sales associates) attending a wide range of events in a wide range of settings. Scenarios may include small, medium, or large settings; urban, suburban, or rural locations; and informal, semi-formal, or formal occasions. Consequently, ETH would like to have three mobile showroom sizes (small, medium, large), along with an employee support and a lavatorial toy hauler. This set of toy haulers will enable ETH to create a variety of configurations and thereby fit in at almost any event anywhere in the US.

When ETH is invited to an event, or receives permission to attend an event, a number of questions will be asked to help ETH determine the best possible mobile showroom configuration for each particular situation:

How many people will be at the event, exhibition, or trade show?

How much square footage is available for the mobile showrooms?

What activities are potential customers participating in at the event, exhibition, or trade show (i.e., weddings, dog shows, motorsport events, etc.)?

Depending on the answers to these questions, ETH will decide which size, and how many, toy hauler showrooms would be best suited for that particular occasion. Consequently, ETH needs configuration options for setting up small, medium, and large toy haulers in a variety of settings. These options are described shortly.

In all situations, ETH drivers will haul the showrooms to each location and set up whatever configuration has been determined to be apprpriate for the occasion and site. Sellers will be flown in to each location. All drivers and sellers will stay in hotels.

End User Profiles and Activities

Table C01 End user profiles and activities

	Quanitity	Gender	Age	Psych needs	Special needs
Primary end users					
Sellers	3–36	M, F	25–60	Security Privacy	Wheelchair & scooter access
Secondary end users					
Customers	1–75	M, F	1–90	Security Safety Comfort	Customers may have mobility, cognitive, visual, or hearing impairments
Drivers	1–12	M, F	30–65	Safety	

End User Activity Analysis

Seller Typical Day When on the Road

Update knowledge about company products

Research RV and toy hauler trends

Review social media to see what people are looking for in toy haulers

Review sales material (how to be a better seller, etc.)

Prepare for upcoming events (weddings, races, trade shows, etc.)

Seller Typical Day When at an Event

  Breakfast at local restaurant

  Set up showroom, dust, replenish brochures, etc.

  Greet people, answer questions, design toy haulers with customers, write up
    sales agreement

  Close down showroom for evening

  Wind down, read, shower, sleep

Driver Typical Day When on the Road

  Drive sellers to next event

  Fix minor problems with toy hauler showrooms

  Eat

  Sleep

Driver Typical Day When at an Event

  Stay close by in case sellers need assistance or a toy hauler needs repairs

  Show interested customers some of the mechanical features of the toy haulers

  At end of event, clean out grey and black water tanks

Customer Activities

  Read, observe

  Ask questions, talk

  Drink

  Use washroom

  Design toy hauler

  Purchase toy hauler

  Touch, feel, experience

  Learn about inside, outside, features, technology, etc.

  Could spend as little as 5 minutes and as much as 5 hours

Activity Analysis Summary

An analysis of end-user activities revealed the following:

  Sellers and drivers will need to use the employee support toy hauler at
numerous times throughout the day whether it be for coffee breaks, preparing lunch

or dinner, napping, taking a quick shower, or changing clothes. Consequently, the employee support toy hauler will need to house a wide range of employee activities. Additionally, both sellers and drivers will need a secure place for a small number of personal belongings.

When customers are not in the showrooms, sellers will use the showrooms to research toy hauler trends, catch up on paperwork, or prepare for upcoming events. As such, employee work surfaces and seating should allow for long hours of work.

Customers can spend up to five hours with a seller while configuring a custom toy hauler. Therefore, customer seating needs to be particularly comfortable. Additionally, ETH may want to have on hand, a variety of small beverages and snacks to sustain customers throughout the long design process. And, customers, who are in the showrooms for any length of time, may need to use a washroom.

Customers will want to have first-hand experience with the materials and craftsmanship that they can expect in their own toy hauler. As such, each showroom should have samples on hand of all of the available finishes, and the showrooms themselves should exhibit fine craftsmanship.

Toy Hauler Data Sheets

Small Travel Trailer

    21' long | 8' wide | 8' ceiling height | 202 ft²

    3–4 sellers

    2–3 customers

FF&E: Employee and customer seating, two work surfaces for AR and VR design and sales, wall or table or shelf for brochures, tablets for each employee and three for the public, large monitors where customers can see their custom designed toy hauler, projector, white wall as screen

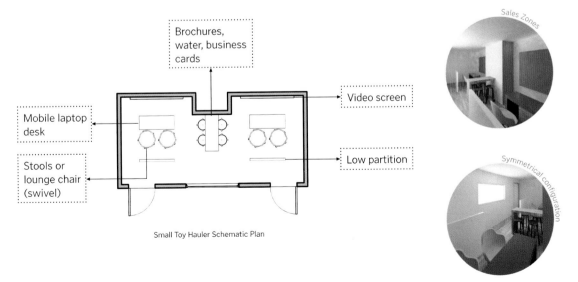

SEATING & DESK AREA

SALES ZONE

SALES ZONE

——— Primary Circulation
········· Secondary Circulation

ENTRY

ENTRY

Outside view

Small Toy Hauler Zoning and Circulation

Schematic Concepts

Brochures, water, business cards

Video screen

Mobile laptop desk

Low partition

Stools or lounge chair (swivel)

Small Toy Hauler Schematic Plan

Sales Zones

Symmetrical configuration

Figure C03 Small travel trailer toy hauler data sheet

Large Fifth Wheel

41' long | 8'-6" wide | 8'-6" ceiling height | 417 ft²

4–6 sellers

1–8 customers

FF&E: Employee and customer seating, work surface for AR and VR design and sales, wall or table or shelf for brochures, laptops for each employee and three for the public, large monitors where customers can see their custom designed toy hauler, projector, white wall as screen

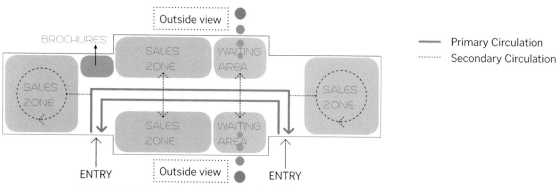

Image 4. Zoning and circulation diagram of the large toy hauler.

Schematic Concepts

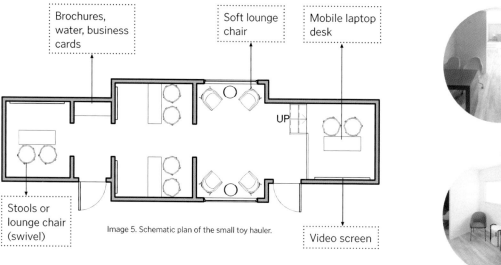

Image 5. Schematic plan of the small toy hauler.

Figure C04 Large fifth wheel toy hauler data sheet

Class A

39'-9" long | 8' wide | 8' ceiling height | 386 ft^2

6–8 sellers

1–12 customers

FF&E: Employee and customer seating, work surface for AR and VR design and sales, wall or table or shelf for brochures, laptops for each employee and three for the public, large monitors where customers can see their custom designed toy hauler, projector, white wall as screen

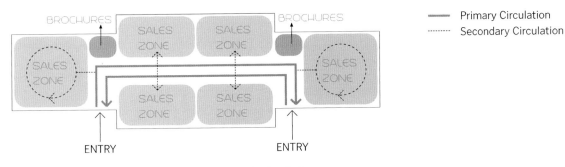

Image 6. Zoning and circulation diagram of the class A toy hauler.

Schematic Concepts

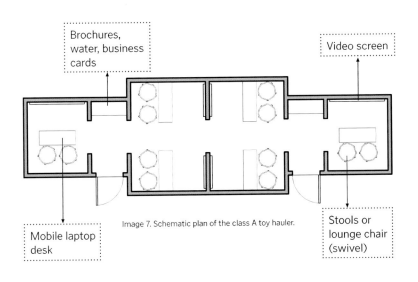

Image 7. Schematic plan of the class A toy hauler.

Figure C05 Class A toy hauler data sheet

Employee Support

38' long | 8' wide | 8' ceiling height | 375 ft²

6–8 sellers and/or drivers

FF&E: Washroom with shower, lounge seating for six, table seating for six, 6–8 lockers for personal belongings

Refrigerator, microwave, sink, dish and utensil storage

Coffee, tea, etc.

Television, stereo system

Work surface

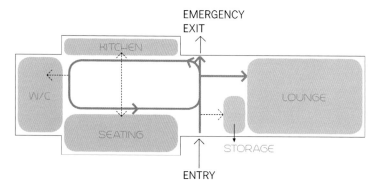

Image 8. Zoning and circulation diagram of the employee support toy hauler.

Schematic Concepts

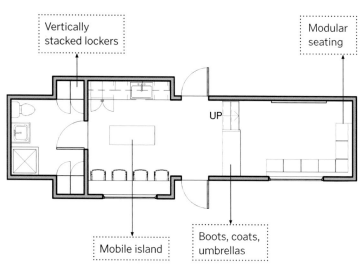

Image 9. Schematic plan of the employee support toy hauler.

Figure C06 Employee support toy hauler data sheet

Lavatorial

39'-9" long | 8' wide | 8' ceiling height | 386 ft²

One men's washroom, one women's washroom, and one family washroom

Separate storage space for toiletries and cleaning supplies

FF&E: Benches for each washroom, seating for six people, automated lavatories, water closets (with automated flush), shelves or tables for towels and toiletries

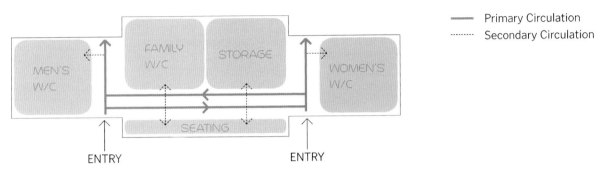

Image 10. Zoning and circulation diagram of the class A toy hauler.

Schematic Concepts

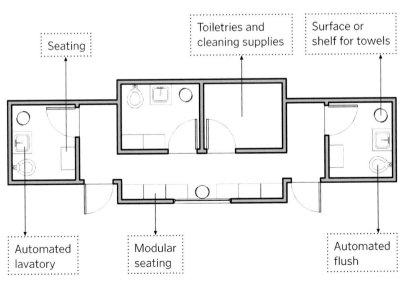

Image 11. Schematic plan of the class A toy hauler.

Figure C07 Lavatorial toy hauler data sheet

Site Configuration Options

The Strip

5,352 ft²

Two large fifth wheel, employee support, and lavatorial toy haulers

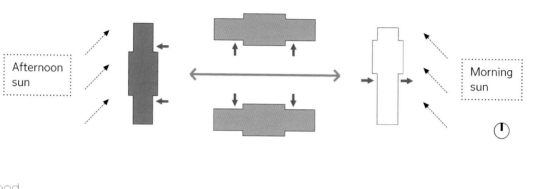

Legend

→ Main Circulation Path
→ Toy Hauler Entry
⋯→ Sun Path

▨ Small Toy Hauler
▨ Large Toy Hauler
▨ Class A Toy Hauler

☐ Employee Support Toy Hauler
■ Lavatorial Toy Hauler

Figure C08 The strip configuration

The Square

3,820 ft²

Small travel trailer, employee support, and lavatorial toy haulers

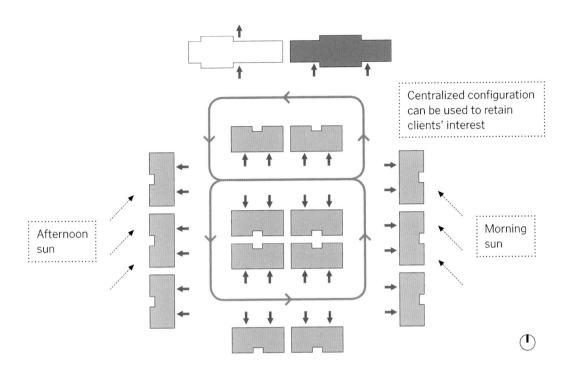

Centralized configuration can be used to retain clients' interest

Afternoon sun

Morning sun

Main Circulation Path
Toy Hauler Entry
Sun Path

Small Toy Hauler
Large Toy Hauler
Class A Toy Hauler

Employee Support Toy Hauler
Lavatorial Toy Hauler

Figure C09 The square configuration

The U-Shape

20,300 ft²

Three large fifth wheel, three small travel trailer, two class A, employee support, and lavatorial toy haulers

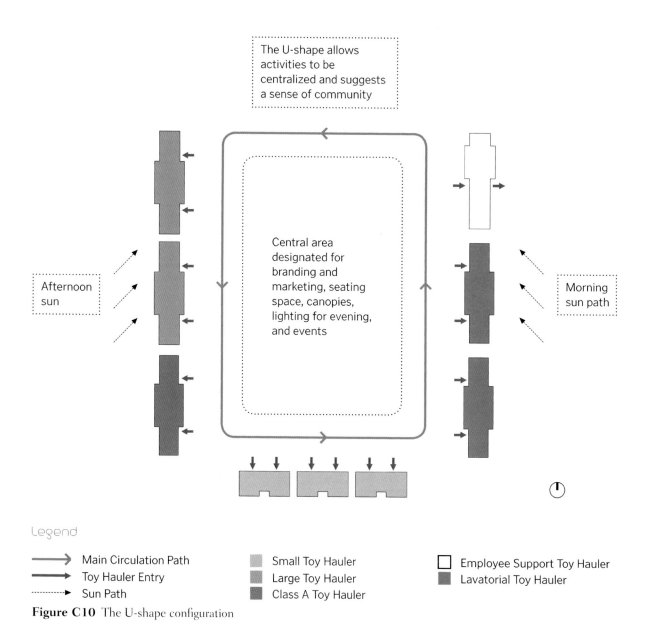

The U-shape allows activities to be centralized and suggests a sense of community

Central area designated for branding and marketing, seating space, canopies, lighting for evening, and events

Afternoon sun

Morning sun path

Legend

→ Main Circulation Path
→ Toy Hauler Entry
·······► Sun Path

Small Toy Hauler
Large Toy Hauler
Class A Toy Hauler

☐ Employee Support Toy Hauler
■ Lavatorial Toy Hauler

Figure C10 The U-shape configuration

Design Guidelines

Based on the project objectives and the client's long-term goals, the following issues were identified as being essential for the success of this project. These unique issues are intended to assist the design team in achieving the client's goals, but are in no way meant to restrict the designers' creativity.

Issue: Innovation

Objective: Each showroom should incorporate innovative technology wherever possible.

Concept: Consider using innovative features wherever possible (e.g., window coverings, door locks, seating, etc.).

Concept: Consider automatic lifts (for wheelchairs, scooters).

Concept: Consider "home automation" technology for controlling lighting, window coverings, etc.

Concept: Consider installing a security system that can be monitored remotely.

Issue: Craftsmanship

Objective: Each showroom should exhibit top quality materials, surfaces, products, and craftsmanship.

Concept: Consider using high end finishes, beautiful joinery, and exquisitely crafted furniture and case goods in each showroom including the employee support toy hauler.

Issue: Brand Identity

Objective: Each showroom, and the exterior areas between the showrooms, should demonstrate ETH's commitment to function, durability, and customization.

Concept: Consider including displays of material choices for furniture, case goods, wall finishes, etc.

Concept: Consider including branded "giveaways" such as water bottles, brochures, notepads, pens, and toys models.

Concept: Consider having three dimensional printers in each showroom so each customer can take away a model of the toy hauler that they designed with their seller.

Issue: *Immersive Retail Experience*

Objective: As a whole, each showroom configuration should make customers feel like they have entered a special world where every indulgence can be accommodated.

Concept: Consider displaying highly functional, interactive, three dimensional toy hauler models outside each showroom to enable customers first-hand experience with ETH's products.

INDEX

Note: Page numbers in **bold** refer to tables and in *italics* to figures.